ROBERT BURNS

First published in Great Britain in 1999 by Brockhampton Press
a member of the Hodder Headline Group
20 Bloomsbury Street, London WC1B 3QA

ISBN 1-86019-9666

A copy of the CIP data is available from the
British Library upon request.

Designed and produced for Brockhampton Press
by Keith Pointing Design Consultancy.

Reprographics by Global Colour
Printed in Singapore.

Robert Burns(1759-96) by Alexander Nasmyth (1758-1840),
Scottish National Portrait Gallery, Edinburgh,
Scotland/Bridgeman Art Library, London/ New York, page 4

The Parting of Robert Burns and his Mary, 1844
by Charles Lucy (1814-73) Malcolm Innes Gallery London, UK/
Bridgeman Art Library, London/ New York, page 87

Front cover illustration, Ellisland on the banks of the Nith,
near Dumfries, a favourite walk of Burns.

# ROBERT BURNS

## A BIOGRAPHY WITH SELECTED POEMS

SASHA BEHAR

BROCKHAMPTON PRESS
LONDON

ROBERT BURNS

'For a Scotsman to see Burns simply as a poet

is well-nigh an impossibility…

He is more a personage to us than a poet,

more a figurehead than a personage,

and more myth than a figurehead…'

FROM ONE SCOTTISH POET to another, these are the words of Edwin Muir in acknowledgement of the man, who within the space of the last three centuries, has become 'poet', 'figurehead' and 'myth', Robert Burns. Statues have been raised in his memory. His verse has been translated into all the major languages of the world and his birthday is celebrated religiously each year on 25 January, Burns Night. So how did a poor farmer's son, from rural Ayrshire, a man who had published really only one book of verse and died, a humble exciseman in Dumfries, at the age of thirty seven, become so revered? His journey is a curious one and has certainly as much to do with Scotland's complex relationship with England as with the undoubted powers and personality of the man himself. As Muir has also pointed out, when Burns was born, Scotland was looking for something. It desperately needed an identifying feature. First the monarchy and then parliament had moved to England and Union in 1707 was reinforced by the decisive defeat at Culloden of Bonnie Prince Charlie. Even the indigenous 'middle Scots' and Gaelic languages were giving way to the English of the South. There were very few poets with either the patronage or the assurance to make what was fast becoming the vernacular into an acceptable literary

MURRAY'S MONUMENT

language. Into this void came a man supposedly untutored, a natural Scottish product to rival the best that England had to offer, an authentic Scottish voice. If Scotland had been looking for something, they had most definitely found it.

Events were also unfolding dramatically overseas. Burns was seventeen when the Continental Congress carried the American Declaration of Independence, and thirty when Parisians sacked the Bastille. Suddenly there were signs of a universal revolt against a feudal or class system. *A mans a man for a' that* Burns was to write, as the American Declaration of Independence made the rights of each individual to life, liberty and the pursuit of happiness legally binding. He was a man in tune with his times. As a farmer with great natural gifts, 'the heaven-taught ploughman', he became not only a resentful and defeated Scotland's triumphant mascot but also over the years, the perfect champion for the bids of emergent democratic societies. This goes a little way to explaining Burns' near mythic status but to understand the man himself is more of a task.

Burns was born in 1759, in Ayrshire, in a village called Alloway a few hundred yards from Alloway Church, which has been immortalised by the poem Tam o'Shanter. His father, William Burnes (as he spelt the name), had come to Ayrshire from Kinkardineshire where he had been a gardener. Apparently he was forced to move on in the aftermath of the 1745 Jacobite rebellion and although he had been reluctant to move, was soon working as head gardener on the estate of a wealthy local Doctor and had met and married a local farmers daughter Agnes Broun. When Burns was six years old, his father wishing to 'keep his children under his own eye till they could discern between good and evil', left his position as gardener and leased the farm of Mount Oliphant, at a very uneconomic rent. It seems obvious now that the lease was no bargain but William Burnes cannot easily be blamed for his choices, as this was a transitional period for Scottish farming and the rise in rents in anticipation of improvement rarely matched the improvement actually completed. Indeed, Burns' father was noted for his

A SHEPHERD

character and intelligence. It was very important to him to give his children as good an education as his means would afford and it was recorded in 1811, in the Agricultural Report on Ayrshire that 'An extensive acquaintance with the mysterious, abstruse and disputed points of systematic divinity, was the species of knowledge farmers generally sought after and to which the greatest fame was attached.' Burns' mother was by contrast barely literate but she played her part in his early education with a store of Scottish songs Burns credits with spurring his initial interest in poetry. In addition, an 'old maid', a friend of his mothers, often came to visit and Burns says of her in an autobiographical letter to a friend, Dr Moore, 'She had, I suppose, the largest collection in the county of tales and songs concerning devils, ghosts, fairies, brownies, witches, warlocks, spunkies, kelpies, elf-candles, deadlights, wraiths, apparitions, cantraips, giants, enchanted towers, dragons and other trumpery. This cultivated the latent seeds of Poesy.'

By now Robert had a younger brother Gilbert and their first real formal education was at the hands of a young man called John Murdoch. In a letter of 1799 Murdoch says 'My pupil Robert Burns, was then (1765) between six and seven years of age; In reading, dividing words into syllables by rule, spelling without book, parsing sentences, etc, Robert and Gilbert were generally at the upper end of the class, even when ranged with boys by far their seniors'. It is not particularly surprising to find that both boys were very bright. What is unexpected is that 'Gilbert always appeared to me to possess a more lively imagination and to be more of the wit, than Robert... if any person who knew the two boys, had been asked which of them was most likely to court the  muses, he would surely never have guessed that Robert had a propensity of that kind.' It is also interesting to find from Murdoch that 'the books most commonly used in the school were, the spelling book, the New Testament, the Bible, Mason's  Collection of Prose and Verse, and Fisher's English Grammar…' Mason's (actually Masson's) collection contains passages from Shakespeare, Milton and Dryden as well as the eighteenth century poets, including Thomson, Gray and Shenstone and prose from Addison and Mrs Elizabeth Rowe's Letters Moral and Entertaining. Clearly Burns was well versed in English literature, far more so, officially, than in Scottish literature which he was to study on his own or pick up through the folk tradition. Unfortunately Murdoch only stayed in Alloway for two and a half years and Burns next met up with him in 1773 when he was sent to board with his old schoolmaster 'for the purposes of revising his English grammar that he might be better qualified to instruct his brothers and sisters at home.' This stay too was short-lived though and it was not until 1775 that Burns returned to formal education in Kirkoswald to learn the more vocational pursuits of 'Mensuration, Surveying, Dialling etc.' By his own admission he got on rather well but he was sixteen now and it was as important to him that he learnt 'to look unconcernedly on a large tavern-bill and mix without fear in a drunken squabble.' Also like any other teenager, he fell in love 'with a charming fillette…who overset my trigonometry and set me off in a tangent from the sphere of my studies.'

Between these intervals of escape for study, Burns was working hard on the farm and education was more haphazard. William

ON THE BLADNOCH

Burnes and other locals made sure that there were books available which Robert apparently read 'with an avidity and industry scarcely to be equalled' but life as a poor farmer's son was exhausting and dispiriting. His brother Gilbert describes it:

> 'We lived very sparingly. For several years butcher's meat was a stranger
> in the house, while all the members of the family exerted themselves to
> the utmost of their strength, and rather beyond, in the labours of the farm.
> My brother… at fifteen was the principal labourer on the farm… I doubt
> not but the hard labour and sorrow of this period of his life, was in a

A COUNTRY WOMAN

great measure the cause of that depression of spirits with which Robert was so often afflicted through his whole life afterwards. At this time he was almost constantly afflicted in the evenings with a dull headache, which at a future period of his life, was exchanged for a palpitation of the heart, and a threatening of fainting and suffocation in his bed, in the night time.'

It was around this time that Robert first tried his hand at 'poesy'. He freely admits that it was inspired by love, that 'delicious passion, which in spite of acid Disappointment, gin-horse Prudence and book-worm Philosophy, I hold to be the first of human joys, our dearest pleasure here below.' He also points out that he had no further aspiration than to woo his current 'fillette'.

'I was not so presumtive as to imagine that I could make verses like printed ones, composed by men who had Greek and Latin, but my girl sung a song which was said to be composed by a small country laird's son, on one of his father's maids, with whom he was in love; and I saw no reason I might not rhyme as well as he' (Burns letter to Dr Moore).

Indeed Burns was now at an age where he was highly aware of his peers. As was common in the Scottish countryside, he was thrown together with the children of landowners who had much greater prospects, a fact he both resented and used to his advantage. He attended a country dancing school 'to give my manners a brush' and set up the Tarbolton Bachelors' Club in November 1780, a debating society which no doubt allowed him to develop the powers of speech and expression for which he was later much noted. His poetic calling was not yet something he took seriously. As he wrote to Dr Moore:

'Poesy was still a darling walk for my mind, but 'twas only the humour of the hour.'

As Burns moved into young adulthood, life was not to get any more predictable. Some difficult years lay ahead trying to find a reliable living and coping with the misadventures of love, years which were to do nothing to help the 'depression of spirits' that his brother Gilbert ascribed to him. In 1781, Burns fell in love with Alison Begbie, the daughter of a farmer with a small holding. It seems he proposed to her and was rejected but the traditional antidote to heartbreak was freely on hand as the present farm at Lochlie needed more and more work. William Burnes had moved the family to the 130 acre farm in 1777. The rent here though was extortionate and after four years respite, wrangling commenced between the landlord and Burns' father which was to end with a threat of prison only avoided because of William's life threatening ill-health. Robert and Gilbert, under pressure to help their father, decided to rent three acres from him for the cultivation of flax which looked as if it was about to become an important crop in Scotland at the time. To ensure success, in 1781, Robert went to Irvine, a large and bustling seaport, north of Ayr, to learn how to dress flax but circumstances again were to thwart his plans. It was not enough that the flax-dresser to whom he had attached himself was untrustworthy but at a party to see in the new year of 1782, the flax-dresser's wife managed

ROUND LOCH OF THE DUNGEON

to set the premises they worked in on fire with the loss of the whole building and everything in it. Burns returned home 'like a true poet, not worth sixpence'. He did however in the time he spent in Irvine make the acquaintance of an educated sailor Richard Brown, who may have been the first to encourage Burns into consummating his love affairs but who also quite vitally inspired him to return to his poetry. Burns writes to Brown in December 1787:

'You told me on my repeating some verses to you, that you wondered

I could resist the temptation of sending verse of such merit to a

LOCH KEN; LOOKING SOUTH

magazine: 'twas actually this that gave me an idea of my own pieces

which encouraged me to endeavour at the character of a Poet.'

At the same time Burns discovered Robert Fergusson's Scots poems, and as he said in his letter to Dr Moore, was impelled by their quality to string 'anew my wildly-sounding, rustic lyre with emulating vigour.'

Early in 1784, exhausted from legal battles and the unrelenting physical labour William Burnes died a bankrupt. Robert and Gilbert salvaged what they could and moved to a farm at Mossgiel. The rent was reasonable but bad weather for the first four years prevented the brothers capitalising on it. Robert concentrated outside of the farm's demands on a

Commonplace book, which he filled between April 1783 and October 1785 with poems and observations about life and literature. He also continued the pursuit of 'charming fillettes' and his first illegitimate child was born in May 1785 to Elizabeth Paton, a servant in the Burns household. There was no expectation of marriage on Elizabeth's part and the baby girl was brought up by Burns' mother. He did not become seriously involved with anybody until he met Jean Armour, attractive daughter of a master mason of Mauchline. She became pregnant early in 1786 and Burns gave her what was almost certainly a valid marriage certificate but again, events were to conspire against him. By now, Burns had a certain reputation, having at least one illegitimate child. He was outspoken and rebellious but more to the point he was simply an impoverished farmer without any apparent prospects. Jean's parents were horrified and her father's lawyer was instructed to cut out the couple's names from the contract, a fact which should have made no difference under the law but which Burns took as a rejection from Jean. Given that Burns is famous for his womanising it might seem surprising that he should have set such store by marriage but it appears to have been an institution that in sentiment at least he held very dear. In his Epistle to Dr Blacklock he asserts that:

> To make a happy fireside clime
>
> to weans and wife
>
> That's the true pathos and sublime
>
> of human life

Not only however was the blow personal, both he and Jean were now subject to the censor of the Church and in order to atone for their sin, it was expected that they endure a public penance. Burns had already suffered this for his relations with Elizabeth Paton and was to appear three times with Jean. Although he had little choice but to accept the penance, he was fiercely opposed to the power of the Kirk Session, a council of parish elders presided over by the Minister, then Rev William Auld, and made it clear in his ecclesiastical satires that he deplored what he saw as the hypocrisy of Calvinism and regarded many of the Kirk's practices as inimical to the concept of a benign God. Certainly, Burns is unlikely to have forgotten the humiliation of sitting on 'the stool of terror' while being reproved publicly by Daddie Auld:

CARLINGWORK LOCH

'Beware of returning to your sin as some of you have done, like the dog

to its vomit, or like the sow that is washed to her wallowing in the mire.'

(2 Peter 2:22)

As it was, although they could not have known it at the time, Robert was always to return to Jean. This was just the opening chapter in a relationship that did in fact end in marriage but not without much confusion and dissatisfaction both before and after. As a salve to his pride and to drive Jean out of his mind, Burns turned to Mary Campbell, *Highland Mary,* who died young possibly in bearing his child. Very little is known about this affair but it seems from lines written after she died addressed 'To Mary in Heaven', where he talks of meeting her by 'the winding Ayr' to 'live one day of parting love', that it was a subject of much regret for him.

Certainly in the time he spent with her he developed the most radical of his plans yet. He was being pursued by Jean's father who was threatening to have him sent to jail if he did not offer support for his children by her. The farm was offering very little income. Burns needed an escape route. 'You and I will never meet in Britain more' he wrote to a friend, in a rather rash and desperate manner. 'I have orders within three weeks at farthest to repair aboard the Nancy, Captain Smith, from Clyde to Jamaica and to call at Antigua.' How serious he was about emigrating is hard to tell. Three ships on which he was booked left without him but his mood was reckless. 'My gaiety is the madness of the intoxicated criminal under the hands of the executioner...' he wrote to Robert Aitken another friend. In the end a stay of execution was procured and from the most unexpected source.

In early April 1786, Burns made arrangements with the Kilmarnock printer John Wilson to bring out a volume of *Scotch Poems*. He had been writing solidly and with great concentration throughout the latter part of 1785 and the early part of 1786, and was determined to have his work published before he left the country. Much later when his worth had been confirmed, he was to say 'I had pretty nearly as high an idea of myself and my works as I have at this moment' and it would have been a man of great natural confidence who would not have been affected by the attention Burns was about to receive. On 31 July 1786, the now famous Kilmarnock edition, whose title page read *Poems, Chiefly in the Scottish Dialect,* by Robert Burns, was published and to great adulation. It was understandable that it should be popular in local farmhouses and cottages, as many of the poems dealt with the rural life, its inhabitants, trials and joys. That is should be such a triumph with the literati in Edinburgh was completely unexpected. Burns must have been particularly gratified by the support and affirmation of Henry Mackenzie author of *The Man of Feeling,* a book that had greatly influenced him earlier in his life. Mackenzie writes of the Kilmarnock Edition and of Burns in a famous review.

> 'If I am not greatly deceived, I think I may safely pronounce him a genius of
> no ordinary rank. The person to whom I allude is Robert Burns, an Ayrshire
> ploughman, whose poems were some time ago published in a country-town
> in the west of Scotland… I hope I shall not be thought to assume too much,
> if I endeavour to place him in a higher point of view, to call for a verdict of

LOCH DEE

his country on the merit of his works, and to claim for him those honours which their excellence appear to deserve.'

Mackenzie also made a plea on Burns' behalf for a patron and it began to seem advisable that Burns visit Edinburgh himself. It was in this visit that the first of the Burns myths began to emerge, that of the 'unlettered rustic who under the influence of the muse shows signs of genius'. Mackenzie, while insisting that the work needed no excuses, could not resist stressing the fact that Burns was 'an Ayrshire ploughman'. He in fact first coined the phrase, 'the heaven-taught ploughman', that was to come to represent the poet in Edinburgh. There was a great fascination at the time in literary circles with 'the natural genius' since the origin of poetry was believed to be 'spontaneous emotional speech' despite the fact that this view sat rather uneasily with a simultaneous interest in form and style. Burns' education may have been erratic but in certain areas it had been very thorough and he had taken pains to supplement it where he thought necessary. The popular perception of him at the time as a primitive was unfounded. However, he also played his part in perpetuating it. He writes in his preface to the Kilmarnock Edition 'Unacquainted with the necessary requisites for commencing Poet by rule, he sings the sentiments and manners he felt and saw in himself and his rustic compeers around him, in his and their native language.' This is not to say that Burns grovelled. He played his role with pride and if he was remarkable at that time it was in his steadiness, the ease and grace with which he appears to have adventured into a different class. Sir Walter Scott says of his one encounter with him at a salon in Edinburgh.

> 'There was a strong expression of sense and shrewdness in all his lineaments.
> The eye alone, I think, indicated the poetical character and temperament. It was
> large, and of a dark cast, which glowed (I say literally glowed) when he spoke
> with feeling or interest. I never saw such another eye in a human head, though
> I have seen the most distinguished men of my time. His conversation expressed
> perfect self-confidence without the slightest presumption.'

Indeed there were many who made his acquaintance there, who despite their admiration for his poetry, believed it was not the greatest of his gifts. Mrs Maria Riddell, writing of him later in *Mrs Maria Riddell's Memoir Concerning Burns* (published in the Dumfries Journal, August 1796) was one of these.

'For the fact is, even allowing his great and original genius its due tribute of admiration, that poetry (I appeal to all who have had the advantage of being personally acquainted with him) was actually not his forte. Many others perhaps may have ascended to prouder heights in the region of Parnassus, but none certainly ever outshone Burns in the charms - the sorcery I would

THE RIVER AYR

THE SOURCE OF THE DEE

almost call it, of fascinating conversation, the spontaneous eloquence of

social argument, or the unstudied poignancy of brilliant repartee.'

The Edinburgh literati by the sounds of it, were near bewitched by

Burns. In the first two weeks of his visit people were fighting to meet him.

Burns had been a Freemason since June 1781 in the St David Masonic

Lodge of Tarbolton and soon after his arrival in Edinburgh he was

introduced to the Canongate Kilwinning Lodge, the members of which

were in many cases very influential. At a meeting of the Grand Lodge of

Scotland, the master gave the toast, 'To Caledonia, and Caledonia's Bard,

Brother Burns'. He had moved on apace. He was not now just 'the natural

genius' but 'Scotland's natural genius', an appellation, however that can only have made the difficulty he was to have securing a patron even more frustrating for him. It is fair to say retrospectively that the role of 'natural genius' eventually worked against him. Firstly it carried in its wake the suggestion that his poetry was effortless but in addition, it rendered an inteested patron rather redundant if Heaven itself was the poet's source. In some respects this was not altogether unfortunate because if the circle Burns was now mixing in were trying to influence him at all, it was away from his natural and most successful bent, an inspired and energetic use of the Scots dialect, and ironically towards a more elegant, formal and neo-classical style of which he was capable but which rarely produced his most effective work. Mackenzie, in his review of the Kilmarnock Edition, had mourned the fact that the Scots dialect in which Burns wrote would preclude him from fame in England. It was beginning to seem that although the literati had initially hailed him for his credentials as home-grown, he was now being pushed into styles that 'might travel'. Burns however seemed adamant where his strengths lay. Again to Dr Moore he writes:

> 'For my part my first ambition was, and still my strongest wish is, to please
> my Compeers, the rustic Inmate of the hamlet… In a language where Pope
> and Churchill have raised the laugh and Shenstone and Gray drawn the tear…
> I am not vain enough to hope for distinguished poetic fame.'

During this period, Burns was lodging in the Old Town, intent on publishing a second volume of his verse and sounding out the possibility of a job in the Excise. He was also remarkably clear sighted about the true extent at the time of his popularity:

> 'I know very well, the novelty of my character has by far the greatest share in

MOORLAND

the learned and polite notice I have lately got.'

He was also aware of the dangers of his position and admits in a letter to an Ayr Banker 'I tremble lest I should be ruined by being dragged to (sic) suddenly into the glare of polite and learned observation.'

To escape from the pressure, Burns cultivated a less exalted circle of friends in the Old Town. He came to know the two men with whom he would soon travel around Scotland, William Nicol, an infamously harsh Latin master at the High School of Edinburgh, and Robert Ainslie, an amiable law student. He joined the Crochallan Fencibles, a drinking club which met not far from his lodgings and in which the exchange of bawdy was the popular pastime that would not have been as happily received elsewhere. Burns took great pleasure in bawdy and writes to a friend in 1792 of his 'own private collection'. At this point though it was a second edition of his present poems he wanted published. It was one of his more influential admirers, the Earl of Glencairn who introduced him to the not altogether reliable Agent, William Creech. A deal was struck, on the advice of Henry Mackenzie, which given Burns present fame seems disappointing but which at the time was probably very generous. As a result, Burns received much more for the second edition than for the first but it was virtually the only money he was ever to make from his poetry and was not to last him for very long.

The first of Burns' Edinburgh ambitions had been achieved then but the second was proving more elusive. He was having no luck gaining a position in the Excise. The Edinburgh noblesse wanted their famous

ON THE FLEET, GATEHOUSE

ploughman back at the plough but by now there was one thing Burns knew
for certain:

> 'The appellation of, a Scotch Bard, is by far my highest pride; to continue to
> deserve it is my most exalted ambition.'

He determined to travel further around Scotland and familiarise
himself with its features and landmarks. For his first trip, Robert visited the
Border Country, rich as it was in literary and historical significance. He
travelled with his friend Robert Ainslie, and on the return journey visited a
farm that Patrick Miller, an Edinburgh Banker, had offered to lease to him.
Life in Ayrshire was continuing and Jean Armour's parents who before had
been so adamantly and insultingly opposed to Burns were now all in favour

of a marriage, but Burns was not to forget his prior humiliation easily and resisted their advances. He had also by now made the acquaintance of women who were not only attractive to him physically but who could hold their own with him intellectually. This was novel for Burns and was to be the source of some discomfort in the future since his class would ultimately keep him from the women who could fully match him. During his stays in Edinburgh he would have physical affairs with a servant girl, May Cameron and one Jenny Clow, both of whom bore children as a result while conducting a passionate and romantic but epistolary affair with the more cautious grass-widow Agnes McLehose.

At the end of June, Burns set out on another tour, this time to the Argyllshire Highlands at the end of which he once more visited Jean and could not resist becoming involved with her again although he made her swear not to demand marriage. She became pregnant and bore him twins both of whom died soon after they were born. Back in Edinburgh Burns was having trouble with his publisher Creech who was not forthcoming with his payment. He was eventually paid after provoking Creech with an angry letter but from the subsequent publication of a two volume edition in 1793, which included at least twenty new poems, among them the narrative masterpiece Tam o'Shanter, he received nothing but a few complementary copies.

Again Burns was off on his travels. On 25 August, 1787, he visited the Highlands, this time with William Nicol, the Edinburgh Schoolmaster. The tour included a visit to Cawdor Castle where Macbeth murdered King

Duncan. 'Saw the bed in which King Duncan was stabbed,' remembers Burns like any other gratified tourist. It was a disappointment though that he had to refuse an offer of hospitality from the Duke and Duchess of Gordon. His companion, William Nicol in Burns' words 'a strong in-kneed sort of a soul', fell into a fury because the invitation had not initially included him and determined to leave immediately, with or without Burns. Regretfully and in some embarassment, Burns joined Nicol. He never saw the Gordons again. Furthermore the same thing had happened at Blair Athole, only on this occasion he was dragged away from the company of Robert Graham of Fintry, Commissioner of Excise, the man he most needed to cultivate, and just missed altogether the visit of Henry Dundas,

THE COURAN LANE

'King Harry the Ninth', one of the most powerful men in Scotland. Burns' attitude to the rich was admittedly ambiguous. In his poems he often put the 'honest' man above the titled rogue, ('the honest man, thoe'er sae poor, Is King o men for a' that') but he was prepared to admit that honesty might be found among the titled as well. In his position, anyway, he could not afford the luxury of opinion. He needed the patronage that the rich could offer.

The social and political advantages of this tour were not the only attractions, however. In this, the most extensive of his tours, Burns was forging a powerful link with the country and landscape he intended to represent in his verse and his attention to it is evident in the songs he went on to collect and write. They are all grounded in the place from which they came. They are localised and specific, and this detail lends them much of their power. The Ayrshire ploughman was deliberately and quite literally broadening his horizons. He set off again on 16 September and on this occasion, spent some time with a gentleman farmer, Mr Chalmers, whose daughter Peggy became swiftly the object of Burns' ardent and serious attentions. She was undoubtedly an intelligent and accomplished young woman and could have been a match for him but she confessed to the poet Thomas Campbell sometime afterwards that, although Burns had proposed, she had felt it necessary to reject him. This must have been further proof to Burns that the women he felt could match him imaginatively and intellectually were unlikely ever to agree to marry him. Whether or not these were Peggy's reasons it would have been clear to her that Burns was still, his reputation with women aside and despite his celebrity, a man without a secure living.

Back in Edinburgh, finding a means of living was becoming a primary concern. A year after his arrival, he was no longer quite the novelty that he had been and he had no desire to return to Mossgiel, the farm which Gilbert had now taken over, so it was probably with some relief that he welcomed the next stage of his literary career. The previous April he had met James Johnson, a man who had invented a cheap process for printing music and was intent on collecting and publishing a volume of Scottish Songs. Burns was asked on his return from the tours to help with the collection, and must have felt events were coming full circle. He could not but have been put in mind of his mother and her 'old maid' friend and he was actually to spend the best part of the rest of his literary life in the collection, writing and editing of the Scottish folk song. While this may appear to have been a loss in some respects, it was eminently suited to his talents and he was devoted to the cause. Furthermore the political events of the time were making it dangerous for a man to be too honest in print and would therefore anyway have circumscribed his more satirical output.

Burns had on various occasions made his sympathies for the French Revolutionaries known. Most famously in 1792 it is said that on seizing the smuggling brig Rosamond in the Solway estuary as exciseman in Dumfries, he purchased from the contents four corronades and sent them to the French, a flamboyant gesture that seems in character. He also rather imprudently wrote a letter to a friend Mrs Dunlop in 1795 which he should

THE CARSPHAIRN HILLS

have anticipated would abruptly end their correspondence, in which he referred to Marie Antoinette and Louis XVI as 'a perjured blockhead and an unprincipled Prostitute'. These views, only just acceptable when expressed in private in the early days of the revolution, were seen as downright seditious later when a French invasion was threatened. Burns was forced to backtrack and it was becoming clear that freedom of expression, although dear to the Americans, was not only disapproved of but positively dangerous in Scotland. The Scottish songs were relatively safe ground for him to exercise his talents and to consolidate his less controversial reputation as Scots Nationalist.

Burns refused to take any money for the work he did over several years first for Johnson on the Scots Musical Museum and later for

George Thomson who required help in his collection of Select Scottish Airs. He pointed out: 'As to any remuneration, you may think my Songs either above, or below price for they shall absolutely be the one or the other.' It was still then pressing for him that he find materially rewarding employment but he was distracted from this in December 1787 by the relationship mentioned earlier that was in principally epistolary form to absorb him for the whole winter. The letters are famous as expressions of Burns' skill and wit and record the passionate course of a love affair it seems was never consummated between 'Clarinda' and her 'Sylvander'. The 'Clarinda' in question was a Mrs Agnes Mc'Lehose, a woman married very young and now separated from her husband. To begin with, the pair wrote not only daily but sometimes hourly to each other so it is baffling that by the end of the winter, early in 1788, Burns was at the same time seeing his first love

CLARINDA

again, Jean Armour. In addition, although he wrote of her in the most disparaging terms to his friends and 'Clarinda', by April to everyone's surprise he had acknowledged her as his wife. Jean had always been loyal and was very tolerant of Burns' affairs even bringing some of his illegitimate children up as her own. The convoluted course of their relationship had finally come to some resolution.

Now that Burns was married, he decided after all to rent the farm in Ellisland offered him by Patrick Miller which he had visited on his first tour. Despite having received his excise instructions, he was not actually to get a job as an Exciseman until September 1789 but when he did it must have come as a huge relief for, as in the past, the farm was quickly proving a ruinous bargain. As soon as he could (1791), Burns left it behind and moved the whole family to Dumfries for what must have seemed like a new beginning. He would still sink into the depressive moods that had hounded him all his life and he was always to find himself positioned uneasily and irreconcilably between two classes but he worked hard as an exciseman and gained the respect and sympathy of his superiors. He was surrounded by friends and had already been made Honorary Burgess in June 1787. The family tradition in education continued. James Gray, a Dumfries school teacher, describes a visit he made to the Burns' household where he found Robert at home reading and explaining to his children the English poets from Shakespeare to Gray. Sadly, although life appeared more settled, the steady wage of the exciseman was earned at some cost. Burns was being required to ride about in all weathers on bad roads and despite his relative youth, his health inevitably deteriorated. By the middle of 1796, it was clear to him and those that knew him, that his rheumatic condition was going to be fatal.

There is some controversy about Burns' drinking habits and how far they contributed to his early death. For some the continual reference to 'drunken squabbles' and his poetic espousal of 'scotch drink', his constant remorseful apologies to friends and the guilt he so often felt after a drinking bout ('the horrors of penitence, regret, remorse, head-ache, nausea, and all the rest of the damned hounds of hell, that beset a poor wretch, who has been guilty of the sin of drunkenness') indicated a tendency if not to alcoholism, certainly to bout-alcoholism. For others, it was simply the habit of the day, compounded by his being a man, a farmer and a Scot. Certainly the physical hardship and the uncertainty of his life would have been enough to bring him early to serious ill health. He died on the 21 July 1796, at the age of thirty seven, three days after expressing in the last letter he was ever to write, concern for his heavily pregnant wife and, strangely, a presentiment of his death.

Burns was a contradictory figure then, a man caught on the cusp of a new era historically, between literary traditions, and because of his 'genius' between classes. No wonder to use the words of Byron, he developed such an 'antithetical mind, tenderness, roughness - delicacy, coarseness - sentiment, sensuality - soaring and grovelling, dirt and deity - all mixed up in that one compound of inspired clay'. There is no lack of material to fuel the 'myth' and indeed he has been moulded to not just one but many

LOCH CHESNEY

different forms over time, the drinker's Burns, the womaniser's Burns, the Scot's Burns, the socialist's Burns, the democrat's Burns. There is a certain irony though, in the fact, that a poet who so often in his lifetime lamented he would never be able to withstand 'the full glare of learned and polite observation', is now so often of more interest because of his habits than his poetry. Of the Burns nights, Hugh McDiarmid had said in the poem *A Drunk Man Looks At a Thistle* (1926) 'No' wan in fifty kens a wurd Burns wrote.' Edwin Muir as well regrets that it is almost impossible to see Burns first and foremost as a poet. Maybe this is an apt place to conclude then – that in the face of Burns contradictory life and personality it is best to look simply to the poems and seek the man there.

## TAM O' SHANTER

When chapman billies leave the street,
And drouthy neibors neibors meet;
As market-days are wearing late,
An' folk begin to tak the gate;
While we sit bousing at the nappy,
An' getting fou and unco happy,
We think na on the lang Scots miles,
The mosses, waters, slaps and styles,
That lie between us and our hame,
Where sits our sulky, sullen dame,
Gathering her brows like gathering storm,
Nursing her wrath to keep it warm.
  This truth fand honest Tam o' Shanter,
As he frae Ayr ae night did canter -
(Auld Ayr, wham ne'er a town surpasses
For honest men and bonnie lasses).
  O Tam! hadst thou but been sae wise
As ta'en thy ain wife Kate's advice!
She tauld thee weel thou was a skellum,
A bletherin', blusterin', drunken blellum;
That frae November till October,

Ae market-day thou was na sober;
That ilka melder wi' the miller
Thou sat as lang as thou had siller;
That every naig was ca'd a shoe on,
The smith and thee gat roarin' fou on;
That at the Lord's house, even on Sunday,
Thou drank wi' Kirkton Jean till Monday.
She prophesied that, late or soon,
Thou would be found deep drown'd in Doon;
Or catch'd wi' warlocks in the mirk
By Alloway's auld haunted kirk.

Ah, gentle dames! it gars me greet
To think how mony counsels sweet,
How mony lengthen'd sage advices.
The husband frae the wife despises!

But to our tale: Ae market night,
Tam had got planted unco right,
Fast by an ingle, bleezing finely,
Wi' reaming swats, that drank divinely;
And at his elbow, Souter Johnny,
His ancient, trusty, drouthy crony;
Tam lo'ed him like a very brither;
They had been fou for weeks thegither
The night drave on wi' sangs and clatter;
And aye the ale was growing better:
The landlady and Tam grew gracious,
Wi' favours secret, sweet, and precious;
The souter tauld his queerest stories;
The landlord's laugh was ready chorus:
The storm without might rair and rustle,
Tam did na mind the storm a whistle.

Care, mad to see a man sae happy,

E'en drown'd himsel amang the nappy.
As bees flee hame wi' lades o' treasure,
The minutes wing'd their way wi' pleasure;
Kings may be blest, but Tam was glorious,
O'er a' the ills o' life victorious!

But pleasures are like poppies spread -
You seize the flow'r, its bloom is shed;
Or like the snow falls in the river -
A moment white, then melts for ever;
Or like the borealis race,
That flit ere you can point their place;
Or like the rainbow's lovely form
Evanishing amid the storm.
Nae man can tether time nor tide;
The hour approaches Tam maun ride;
That hour, o' night's black arch the key-stane,
That dreary hour, he mounts his beast in;
And sic a night he taks the road in,
As ne'er poor sinner was abroad in.

The wind blew as 'twad blawn its last;
The rattling show'rs rose on the blast;
The speedy gleams the darkness swallow'd;
Loud, deep, and lang, the thunder bellow'd
That night, a child might understand,
The Deil had business on his hand.

Weel mounted on his gray mare, Meg,
A better never lifted leg,
Tam skelpit on thro' dub and mire,
Despising wind, and rain, and fire;
Whiles holding fast his gude blue bonnet;
Whiles crooning o'er some auld scots sonnet;
Whiles glow'ring round wi' prudent cares,

CREETOWN BAY

Lest bogles catch him unawares.
Kirk-Alloway was drawing nigh,
Whare ghaists and houlets nightly cry.

By this time he was cross the ford,
Where in the snaw the chapman smoor'd;
And past the birks and meikle stane,
Where drunken Charlie brak's neck-bane;
And thro' the whins, and by the cairn,
Where hunters fand the murder'd bairn;
And near the thorn, aboon the well,
Where Mungo's mither hang'd hersel.
Before him Doon pours all his floods;
The doubling storm roars thro' the woods;
The lightnings flash from pole to pole;
Near and more near the thunders roll:
When, glimmering thro' the groaning trees,
Kirk-Alloway seem'd in a bleeze;
Thro' ilka bore the beams were glancing;
And loud resounded mirth and dancing.

Inspiring bold John Barleycorn!
What dangers thou canst make us scorn!
Wi'tippenny, we fear nae evil;
Wi' usquebae, we'll face the devil!
The swats sae ream'd in Tammie's noddle,
Fair play, he car'd na deils a boddle!
But Maggie stood right sair astonish'd,
Till, by the heel and hand admonish'd,
She ventur'd forward on the light;
And, vow! Tam saw an unco sight!
Warlocks and witches in a dance!
Nae cotillon brent new frae France,
But hornpipes, jigs, strathspeys, and reels,

Put life and mettle in their heels.

A winnock-bunker in the east,

There sat auld Nick, in shape o' beast-

A touzie tyke, black, grim, and large!

To gie them music was his charge:

He screw'd the pipes and gart them skirl,

Till roof and rafters a' did dirl.

Coffins stood round like open presses,

That shaw'd the dead in their last dresses;

And by some devilish cantraip sleight

Each in its cauld hand held a light,

By which heroic Tam was able

To note upon the haly table

A murderer's banes in gibbet-airns;

Twa span-lang, wee, unchristen'd bairns;

A thief new-cutted frae the rape -

Wi' his last gasp his gab did gape;

Five tomahawks, with blude red rusted;

Five scymitars, wi' murder crusted;

A garter, which a babe had strangled;

A knife, a father's throat had mangled,

Whom his ain son o' life bereft -

The gray hairs yet stack to the heft;

Wi' mair of horrible and awfu',

Which even to name wad be unlawfu'.

    As Tammie glowr'd, amaz'd, and curious,

The mirth and fun grew fast and furious:

The piper loud and louder blew;

The dancers quick and quicker flew;

They reel'd, they set, they cross'd, they cleekit,

Till ilka carlin swat and reekit,

And coost her duddies to the wark,

And linkit at it in her sark!

    Now Tam, O Tam! had thae been queans,
A' plump and strapping in their teens;
Their sarks, instead o' creeshie flannen,
Been snaw-white seventeen hunder linen!
Thir breeks o' mine, my only pair,
That ance were plush, o' gude blue hair,
I wad hae gi'en them off my hurdies,
For ae blink o' the bonnie burdies!

    But wither'd beldams, auld and droll,
Rigwoodie hags wad spean a foal,
Louping and flinging on a crummock,
I wonder didna turn thy stomach.

    But Tam kent what was what fu' brawlie,
There was ae winsome wench and walie
That night enlisted in the core,
Lang after kent on Carrick shore!
(For mony a beast to dead she shot,
And perish'd mony a bonnie boat,
And shook baith meikle corn and bear,
And kept the country-side in fear.)
Her cutty sark, o' Paisley harn,
That while a lassie she had worn,
In longitude tho' sorely scanty,
It was her best, and she was vauntie.
Ah! little kent thy reverend grannie
That sark she coft for her wee Nannie
Wi' twa pund Scots ('twas a' her riches)
Wad ever grac'd a dance of witches!

    But here my muse her wing maun cour;
Sic flights are far beyond her pow'r -
To sing how Nannie lap and flang

(A souple jade she was, and strang);
And how Tam stood, like ane bewitch'd,
And thought his very een enrich'd
Even Satan glowr'd, and fidg'd fu' fain,
And hotch'd and blew wi' might and main:
Till first ae caper, syne anither,
Tam tint his reason a' thegither,
And roars out "Weel done, Cutty-sark!"
And in an instant all was dark!
And scarcely had he Maggie rallied,
When out the hellish legion sallied.

As bees bizz out out wi' angry fyke
When plundering herds assail their byke.
As open pussie's mortal foes
When pop! she starts before their nose.
As eager runs the market-crowd,
When 'Catch the thief!' resounds aloud,
So Maggie runs; the witches follow,
Wi' mony an eldritch skriech and hollow.

Ah, Tam! ah, Tam! thou'll get thy fairin'!
In hell they'll roast thee like a herrin'!
In vain thy Kate awaits thy comin'!
Kate soon will be a woefu' woman!
Now do thy speedy utmost, Meg,
And win the key-stane o' the brig;
There at them thou thy tail may toss,
A running stream they darena cross.
But ere the key-stane she could make,
The fient a tail she had to shake!
For Nannie, far before the restr,
Hard upon noble Maggie prest,

And flew at Tam wi' furious ettle;
But little wist she Maggie's mettle!
Ae spring brought off her master hale,
But left behind her ain gray tail:
The carlin claught her by the rump,
And left poor Maggie scarce a stump.
  Now, wha this tale o' truth shall read,
Each man and mother's son, take heed;
Whene'er to drink you are inclin'd,
Or cutty-sarks rin in your mind,
Think! ye may buy the joys o'er dear;
Remember Tam o' Shanter's mare.

## SCOTS WHA HAE

*Robert Bruce's Address to his army,*
*before the battle of Bannockburn*

Scots, wha hae wi' Wallace bled,
Scots, wham Bruce has aften led,
Welcome to your gory bed,
  Or to victorie.

Now's the day, and now's the hour;
See the front o' battle lour!
See approach proud Edward's power–
  Chains and slaverie!

Wha will be a traitor knave?
Wha can fill a coward's grave?
Wha sae base as be a slave?
  Let him turn and flee!

Wha for Scotland's King and law
Freedom's sword will strongly draw,
Freeman stand, or freeman fa'?
  Let him follow me!

By oppression's woes and pains!
By your sons in servile chains!
We will drain our dearest veins,
  But they shall free!

Lay the proud usurpers low!
Tyrants fall in every foe!
Liberty's in every blow!
  Let us do or die!

## UP IN THE MORNING

Up in the morning's no' for me,
Up in the morning early;
When a' the hills are cover'd wi' snaw
I'm sure it's winter fairly.

Cauld blaws the wind frae east to west,
The draft is driving sairly;
Sae loud and shrill's I hear the blast,
I'm sure it's winter fairly.

The birds sit chittering in the thorn,
A' day they fare but sparely ;
And lang's the night frae e'en to morn;
I'm sure it's winter fairly.

## DEATH AND DOCTOR HORNBOOK

Some books are lies frae end to end,
And some great lies were never penn'd:
Ev'n ministers, they hae been kenn'd,
       In holy rapture,
A rousing whid at times to vend,
        And nail't wi' Scripture.

But this that I am gaun to tell,
Which lately on a night befell,
Is just as true's the Deil's in hell
       Or Dublin city:
That e'er he nearer comes oursel
        'S a muckle pity.

The Clachan yill had made me canty,
I wasna fou, but just had plenty;
I stacher'd whyles, but yet took tent aye
       To free the ditches;
An' hillocks, stanes, an' bushes kent aye
        Frae ghaists an' witches.

The rising moon began to glowre
The distant Cumnock hills out-owre:
To count her horns, wi' a' my pow'r,
       I set mysel;
But whether she had three or four
        I cou'd na tell.

I was come round about about the hill,
And todlin' down on Willie's mill,
Setting my staff, wi' a' my skill,
                    To keep me sicker;
Tho' leeward whyles, against my will,
                    I took a bicker.

I there wi' Something did forgather,
That pat me in an eerie swither;
An awfu' scythe, out-owre ae shouther,
                    Clear-dangling, hang;
A three-tae'd leister on the ither
                    Lay large an' lang.

Its stature seem'd lang Scotch ells twa,
The queerest shape that e'er I saw,
For fient a wame it had ava;
                    And then its shanks
They were as thin, as sharp an' sma'
                    As cheeks o' branks.

'Guid-een' quo' I; 'Friend! hae ye been mawin,
When ither folk are busy sawin?'
It seem'd to mak a kind o' stan',
                    But naething spak;
At length says I, 'Friend, wh'are ye gaun?
                    Will ye go back?'

It spak right howe - 'My name is Death,
But be na fley'd. - Quoth I, 'Guid faith,
Ye're maybe come to stap my breath;
          But tent me, billie:
I red ye weel, tak care o' skaith,
          See, there's a gully!'

Gudeman' quo' he, 'put up your whittle,
I'm no design'd to try its mettle;
But if I did - I wad be kittle
          To be mislear'd -
I wad na mind it, no that spittle
          Out-owre my beard.'

'Weel, weel!' says I, a bargain be't;
Come, gies your hand, an' sae we're gree't;
We'll ease our shanks an' tak a seat -
          Come, gies your news;
This while ye hae been mony a gate,
          At mony a house.'

'Ay, ay!' quo' he, an' shook his head,
It's e'en a lang lang time indeed
Sin' I began to nick the thread,
          An' choke the breath:
Folk maun do something for their bread,
          An' sae maun Death.

'Sax thousand years are near-hand fled,
Sin' I was to the butching bred;
An' mony a scheme in vain's been laid
   To stap or scaur me;
Till ane Hornbook's ta'en up the trade,
   An' faith! he'll waur me.

'Ye ken Jock Hornbook i' the clachan -
Deil mak his king's-hood in a spleuchan!
He's grown sae well acquaint wi' Buchan
   An' ither chaps,
The weans haud out their fingers laughin',
   And pouk my hips.

'See, here's a scythe, an' there's a dart -
They hae pierc'd mony a gallant heart;
But Doctor Hornbook, wi' his art
   And cursed skill,
Has made them baith no worth a fart!
   Damn'd haet they'll kill.

''Twas but yestreen, nae farther gane,
I threw a noble throw at ane -
Wi' less, I'm sure, I've hundreds slain -
   But deil may care!
It just play'd dirl on the bane,
   But did nae mair.

'Hornbook was by wi' ready art,
And had sae fortified the part
That, when I lookèd to my dart,
   It was sae blunt,
Fient haet o't wad hae pierc'd the heart
   O' a kail-runt.

'I drew my scythe in sic a fury
I near-hand cowpit wi' my hurry,
But yet the bauld Apothecary
   Withstood the shock;
I might as weel hae tried a quarry
   O' hard whin rock.

'E'en them he canna get attended,
Altho' their face he ne'er had kenn'd it,
Just sh – in a kail-blade, and send it,
   As soon's he smells't,
Baith their disease, and what will mend it,
   At once he tells't.

'And then a' doctor's saws and whittles,
Of a' dimensions, shapes, an mettles,
A' kinds o' boxes, mugs, an' bottles,
   He's sure to hae;
Their Latin names as fast he rattles
   As A B C.

'Calces o' fossils, earths, and trees;
True sal-marinum o' the seas;
The farina of beans and pease,
                    He has't in plenty;
Aqua-fontis, what you please,
                    He can content ye.

'Forbye some new uncommon weapons, -
Urinus spiritus of capons;
Or mite-horn shavings, filings, scrapings,
                    Distill'd per se;
Sal-alkali o' midge-tail clippings,
                    And mony mae.'

'Wae's me for Johnie Ged's Hole now,'
Quoth I, 'if that thae news be true!'
His braw calf-ward where gowans grew
                    Sae white and bonnie,
Nae doubt they'll rive it wi' the plew;
                    They'll ruin Johnie!'

The creature grain'd an eldritch laugh,
And says 'Ye needna yoke the pleugh,
Kirk-yards will soon be till'd eneugh,
                    Tak ye nae fear;
They'll a' be trench'd wi' mony a sheugh,
                    In twa-three year.

'Where I kill anc, a fair strae-death,
By loss o' blood or want o' breath,
This night I'm free to tak my aith
         That Hornbook's skill
Has clad a score i' their last claith,
         By drap and pill.

'An honest wabster to his trade,
Whase wife's twa nieves were scarce weel-bred,
Gat tippence-worth to mend her head
         When it was sair;
The wife slade cannie to her bed,
         But ne'er spak mair.

'A country laird had ta'en the batts,
Or some curmurring in his guts,
His only son for Hornbook sets,
         An' pays him well:
The lad, for twa guid gimmer-pets,
         Was laird himsel.

'A bonnie lass, ye kenn'd her name,
Some ill brewn drink had hov'd her wame;
She trusts hersel, to hide the shame,
         In Hornbook's care;
Horn sent her aff to her lang hame,
         To hide it there.

'That's just a swatch o' Hornbook's way;
Thus goes he on from day to day,
Thus does he poison, kill, an' slay,
        An's weel pay'd for't;
Yet stops me o' my lawfu' prey
          Wi' his damn'd dirt.

'But, hark! I'll tell you of a plot,
Tho' dinna ye be speaking o't;
I'll nail the self-conceited sot
        As dead's a herrin':
Niest time we meet, I'll wad a groat,
          He gets his fairin'!

But, just as he began to tell,
The auld kirk-hammer strak the bell
Some wee short hour ayont the twal,
        Which rais'd us baith:
I took the way that pleas'd mysel,
          And sae did Death.

## AE FOND KISS

Ae fond kiss, and then we sever!
Ae fareweel, and then for ever!
Deep in heart-wrung tears I'll pledge thee,
Warring sighs and groans I'll wage thee.
Who shall say that fortune grieves him
While the star of hope she leaves him?
Me, nae cheerfu' twinkle lights me,
Dark despair around benights me.

I'll ne'er blame my partial fancy,
Naething could resist my Nancy;
But to see her was to love her,
Love but her, and love for ever.
Had we never lov'd sae kindly,
Had we never lov'd sae blindly,
Never met – or never parted,
We had ne'er been broken-hearted.

Fare thee weel, thou first and fairest!
Fare thee weel, thou best and dearest!
Thine be ilka joy and treasure,
Peace, enjoyment, love and pleasure.
Ae fond kiss, and then we sever;
Ae fareweel, alas, for ever!
Deep in heart-wrung tears I'll pledge thee,
Warring sighs and groans I'll wage thee.

## TO A MOUSE

*On turning her up in her nest with the plough,*
*November 1785*

Wee, sleekit, cow'rin', tim'rous beastie,
O what a panic's in thy breastie!
Thou need na start awa sae hasty,
         Wi' bickering brattle!
I wad be laith to rin an' chase thee
         Wi' murd'ring pattle!

I'm truly sorry man's dominion
Has broken Nature's social union,
An' justifies that ill opinion
         Which makes thee startle
At me, thy poor earth-born companion,
         An' fellow-mortal!

I doubt na, whiles, but thou may thieve;
What then? poor beastie, thou maun live!
A daimen-icker in a thrave,
         'S a sma' request:
I'll get a blessin' wi' the lave,
         And never miss 't!

Thy wee bit housie, too, in ruin!
Its silly wa's the win's are strewin'!
An' naething, now, to big a new ane,
         O' foggage green!
An' bleak December's winds ensuin',
         Baith snell an' keen!

LOCH KEN; LOOKING NORTH

Thou saw the fields laid bare and waste,
An' weary winter comin' fast,
An' cozie here, beneath the blast,
   Thou thought to dwell,
Till crash! the cruel coulter past
   Out thro' thy cell.

That wee bit heap o' leaves an' stibble
Has cost thee mony a weary nibble!
Now thou 's turn'd out, for a' thy trouble,
   But house or hald,
To thole the winter's sleety dribble,
   An' cranreuch cauld!

But, Mousie, thou art no thy lane,
In proving foresight may be vain:
The best laid schemes o' mice an' men
   Gang aft a-gley,
An' lea'e us nought but grief an' pain
   For promis'd joy.

Still thou art blest compar'd wi' me!
The present only toucheth thee:
But och! I backward cast my e'e
   On propects drear!
An' forward tho' I canna see,
   I guess an' fear!

## THE COTTER'S SATURDAY NIGHT

November chill blaws loud wi' angry sough;
  The short'ning winter-day is near a close;
The miry beasts retreating frae the pleugh;
  The black'ning trains o'craws to their repose:
  The toil-worn Cotter frae his labour goes,
This night his weekly moil is at an end,
  Collects his spades, his mattocks, and his hoes,
Hoping the morn in ease and rest to spend,
And weary, o'er the moor, his course does hameward bend.

At length his lonely cot appears in view,
Beneath the shelter of an agèd tree;
Th' expectant wee things, toddlin', stacher through
  To meet their Dad, wi' flichterin' noise an' glee.
  His wee bit ingle, blinkin bonnilie,
His clean hearth-stane, his thrifty wifie's smile,
  The lisping infant prattling on his knee,
Does a' his weary kiaugh and care beguile,
An' makes him quite forget his labour an' his toil.

Belyve, the elder bairns come drapping in,
  At service out, amang the farmers roun';
Some ca' the pleugh, some herd, some tentie rin
  A cannie errand to a neibor town:
  Their eldest hope, their Jenny, woman-grown,
In youthfu' bloom, love sparkling in her e'e,
  Comes hame, perhaps to shew a braw new gown,
Or deposite her sair-won penny-fee,
To help her parents dear, if they in hardship be.

With joy unfeign'd, brothers and sisters meet,
　An' each for other's weelfare kindly spiers:
The social hours, swift-wing'd, unnoticed fleet;
　Each tells the uncos that he sees or hears;
　The parents, partial, eye their hopeful years;
Anticipation forward points the view.
　The mother, wi' her needle an' her sheers,
Gars auld claes look amaist as weel's the new;
The father mixes a' wi' admonition due.

Their master's an' their mistress's command,
　The younkers a' are warnèd to obey;
An' mind their labours wi' an eydent hand,
　An' ne'er, tho' out o' sight, to jauk or play:
　'And O! be sure to fear the Lord alway,
An' mind your duty, duly, morn an' night!
　Lest in temptation's path ye gang astray,
Implore His counsel and assisting might:
They never sought in vain that sought the Lord aright!'

But hark! a rap comes gently to the door;
　Jenny, wha kens the meaning o' the same,
Tells how a neibor lad cam o'er the moor,
　To do some errands, and convoy her hame.
　The wily mother sees the conscious flame
Sparkle in Jenny's e'e, and flush her cheek;
　Wi' heart-struck anxious care, inquires his name,
While Jenny hafflins is afraid to speak;
Weel-pleased the mother hears it's nae wild worthless rake.

Wi' kindly welcome, Jenny bring him ben;
   A strappin' youth; he takes the mother's eye;
Blythe Jenny sees the visit 's no ill ta'en;
   The father cracks of horses, pleughs, and kye.
   The youngster's artless heart o'erflows wi' joy,
But blate and laithfu', scarce can weel behave;
   The mother, wi' a woman's wiles, can spy
What makes the youth sae bashfu' an' sae grave;
Weel-pleased to think her bairn's respected like the lave .....

But now the supper crowns their simple board,
   The halesome parritch, chief of Scotia's food:
The sowpe their only hawkie does afford,
   That 'yont the hallan snugly chows her cood;
   The dame brings forth in complimental mood,
To grace the lad, her weel-hain'd kebbuck, fell;
   And aft he's prest, and aft he ca's it guid;
The frugal wifie, garrulous, will tell
How 'twas a towmond auld, sin' lint was i' the bell.

The cheerfu' supper done, wi' serious face
   They round the ingle form a circle wide;
The sire turns o'er, wi' patriarchal grace,
   The big ha'-Bible, ance his Father's pride:
   His bonnet rev'rently is laid aside,
His lyart haffets wearing thin an' bare;
   Those strains that once did sweet in Zion glide —
He wales a portion with judicious care,
And 'Let us worship God!' he says with solemn air....

Then homeward all take off their several way;
  The youngling cottagers retire to rest:
The parent-pair their secret homage pay,
  And proffer up to Heav'n the warm request,
  That He who stills the raven's clam'rous nest,
And decks the lily fair in flow'ry pride,
  Would, in the way His wisdom sees the best,
For them and for their little ones provide;
But chiefly, in their hearts with grace divine preside.....

MONREITH

## THE TWA DOGS

'Twas in that place o'Scotland's Isle
That bears the name o' auld King Coil,
Upon a bonnie day in June,
When wearin' through the afternoon,
Twa dogs, that werena thrang at hame,
Forgather'd ance upon a time.

   The first I'll name, they ca'd him Caesar,
Was keepit for his Honour's pleasure;
His hair, his size, his mouth, his lugs,
Shew'd he was nane o' Scotland's dogs,
But whalpit some place far abroad,
Where sailors gang to fish for cod.

   His lockèd, letter'd, braw brass collar,
Shew'd him the gentleman and scholar;
But though he was o'high degree,
The fient a pride, nae pride had he;
But wad hae spent an hour caressin'
E'en wi' a tinkler-gipsy's messan:
At kirk or market, mill or smiddie,
Nae tawted tyke, though e'er sae duddie,
But he wad stan't as glad to see him,
An' stroan't on stanes an' hillocks wi' him.

   The tither was a ploughman's collie,
A rhyming, ranting, raving billie,
Wha for his friend and comrade had him,
And in his freaks had Luath ca'd him,
After some dog in Highland sang,
Was made lang syne–Lord knows how lang.

He was a gash an' faithfu' tyke,
As ever lap a sheugh or dyke;
His honest, sonsie, bawsent face
Aye gat him friends in ilka place.
His breast was white, his tousie back
Weel clad wi' coat o' glossy black;
His gawsie tail, wi' upward curl,
Hung owre his hurdies wi' a swirl.

Nae doubt but they were fain o' ither,
And unco pack and thick thegither;
Wi' social nose whyles snuff'd and snowkit;
Whyles mice and moudieworts they howkit;
Whyles scour'd awa in lang excursion,
And worried ither in diversion;
Until wi' daffin' weary grown,
Upon a knowe they sat them down,
And there began a lang digression
About the lords o' the creation.

CAESAR
I've aften wonder'd, honest Luath,
What sort o' life poor dogs like you have;
An' when the gentry's life I saw,
What way poor bodies liv'd ava.
Our Laird gets in his rackèd rents,
His coals, his kain, and a' his stents;
He rises when he likes himsel';
His flunkies answer at the bell:
He ca's his coach; he ca's his horse;
He draws a bonny silken purse
As lang's my tail, whare, through the steeks,

LOCH SKERROW

The yellow letter'd Geordie keeks.
  Frae morn to e'en it's nought but toiling
At baking, roasting, frying, boiling;
And though the gentry first are stechin',
Yet ev'n the ha' folk fill their pechan
Wi' sauce, ragouts, and sic like trashtrie,
That's little short o'downright wastrie.
Our whipper-in, wee blastit wonner!
Poor worthless elf! it eats a dinner
Better than ony tenant man
His Honour has in a' the lan';
An' what poor cot-folk pit their painch in,
I own it's past my comprehension.

LUATH

Trowth, Caesar, whyles they're fash'd eneugh:
A cotter howkin' in a sheugh,
Wi' dirty stanes biggin' a dyke.
Baring a quarry, and sic like;
Himsel', a wife, he thus sustains,
A smytrie o'wee duddy weans,
And nought but his han' darg to keep
Them right and tight in thack and rape.
  And when they meet wi' sair disasters,
Like loss o' health, or want o' masters,
Ye maist wad think, a wee touch langer,
And they maun starve o' cauld and hunger;
But how it comes, I never kent yet,
They're maistly wonderfu' contented;
An' buirdly chiels and clever hizzies
Are bred in sic a way as this is.

### CAESAR

But then, to see how ye're negleckit,
How huff'd, and cuff'd, and disrespeckit,
Lord, man! our gentry care as little
For delvers, ditchers and sic cattle;
They gang as saucy by poor folk
As I wad by a stinking brock.
 I've noticed, on our Laird's court-day,
An' mony a time my heart's been wae,
Poor tenant bodies, scant o' cash,
How they maun thole a factors's snash;
He'll stamp and threaten, curse and swear,
He'll apprehend them, poind their gear:
While they maun stan', wi' aspect humble,
An' hear it a', an' fear an' tremble!
 I see how folk live that hae riches;
But surely poor folk maun be wretches!

### LUATH

They're no sae wretched's ane wad think;
Though constantly on poortith's brink,
They're sae accustom'd wi' the sight,
The view o't gi'es them little fright.
 Then chance and fortune are sae guided,
They're aye in less or mair provided;
An' though fatigued wi' close employment,
A blink o' rest 's a sweet enjoyment.
 The dearest comfort o' their lives,
Their grushie weans an' faithfu' wives;
The prattling things are just their pride,
That sweetens a' their fireside.
 And whyles twalpenny-worth o' nappy

Can mak the bodies unco happy;
They lay aside their private cares
To mind the Kirk and State affairs:
They'll talk o' patronage and priests,
Wi' kindling fury i' their breasts;
Or tell what new taxation 's comin',
And ferlie at the folk in Lon'on.

  As bleak-faced Hallowmas returns
They get the jovial rantin' kirns,
When rural life of ev'ry station
Unite in common recreation;
Love blinks, Wit slaps, and social Mirth
Forgets there's Care upo' the earth.

  That merry day the year begins
They bar the door on frosty win's;
The nappy reeks wi' mantling ream,
And sheds a heart-inspiring steam;
The luntin' pipe and sneeshin'-mill
Are handed round wi' right gude-will;
The canty auld folks crackin' crouse,
The young anes ranting through the house–
My heart has been sae fain to see them
That I for joy hae barkit wi' them.

  Still it's owre true that ye hae said,
Sic game is now owre aften play'd.
There's mony a creditable stock
O' decent, honest, fawsont folk,
Are riven out baith root and branch
Some rascal's pridefu' greed to quench,
Wha thinks to knit himsel the faster
In favour wi' some gentle master,
Wha, aiblins, thrang a-parliamentin',
For Britain's guid his saul indentin–

CAESAR

Haith, lad, ye little ken about it;
For Britain's guid!–guid faith! I doubt it!
Say rather, gaun as Premiers lead him,
And saying ay or no's they bid him!
At operas and plays parading,
Mortgaging, gambling, masquerading.
Or maybe, in a frolic daft,
To Hague or Calais taks a waft,
To make a tour, an, tak a whirl,
To learn *bon ton* an' see the worl'.
   There, at Vienna, or Versailles,
He rives his father's auld entails;
Or by Madrid he takes the rout,
To thrum guitars and fecht wi' nowt;
Or down Italian vista startles,
Whore-hunting amang groves o' myrtles;
Then bouses drumly German water,
To make himsel' look fair and fatter,
And clear the consequential sorrows,
Love-gifts of Carnival signoras.
   For Britain's guid!–for her destruction!
Wi' dissipation, feud, and faction!


LUATH

   Hech man! dear sirs! is that the gate
They waste sae mony a braw estate?
Are we sae foughten and harass'd
For gear to gang that gate at last?
   O would they stay aback frae courts,
An' please themselves wi' countra sports,
It wad for ev'ry ane be better,

The laird, the tenant, an' the cotter!
For thae frank, rantin', ramblin' billies,
Fient haet o' them 's ill-hearted fellows:
Except for breakin' o' their timmer,
Or speaking lightly o' their limmer,
Or shootin' o' a hare or moor-cock,
The ne'er-a-bit they're ill to poor folk.
  But will ye tell me, Master Caesar,
Sure great folk's life's a life o' pleasure?
Nae cauld nor hunger e'er can steer them
The vera thought o't needna fear them.

CAESAR

Lord, man, were ye but whyles where I am,
The gentles ye wad ne'er envy 'em.
  It's true, they needna starve or sweat,
Thro' winter's cauld or simmer's heat;
They've nae sair wark to craze their banes,
An' fill auld age wi' grips an' granes:
But human bodies are sic fools,
For a' their colleges and schools,
That when nae real ills perplex them,
They make enow themselves to vex them,
An' aye the less they hae to sturt them,
In like proportion, less will hurt them.
  A country fellow at the pleugh,
His acre's till'd, he's right eneugh;
A country girl at her wheel,
Her dizzen's done, she's unco weel;
But gentlemen, an' ladies warst,
Wi' ev'ndown want o' wark are curst.
They loiter, lounging, lank, and lazy;

Though de'il haet ails them, yet uneasy;
Their days insipid, dull and tasteless;
Their nights unquiet, lang, and restless.
   And ev'n their sports, their balls, and races,
Their galloping through public places;
There's sic parade, sic pomp and art,
The joy can scarely reach the heart.
   The men cast out in party matches,
Then sowther a' in deep debauches:
Ae night they're mad wi' drink and whoring,
Neist day their life is past enduring.
   The ladies arm-in-arm, in clusters,
As great and gracious a' as sisters;
But hear their absent thoughts o' ither,
They're a' run de'ils and jads thegither.
Whyles, owre the wee bit cup and platie,
They sip the scandal-potion pretty;
Or lee-lang nights, wi' crabbit leuks,
Pore owre the devil's pictur'd beuks;
Stake on a chance a farmer's stack-yard,
And cheat like ony unhang'd blackguard.
   There's some exceptions, man and woman;
But this is gentry's life in common.

   By this the sun was out o' sight,
And darker gloamin brought the night;
The bum-clock humm'd wi' lazy drone,
The kye stood rowtin' i' the loan;
When up they gat and shook their lugs,
Rejoiced they werena men but dogs;
And each took aff his several way,
Resolved to meet some ither day.

## CONTENTED WI' LITTLE

Contented wi' little, and cantie wi' mair,
Whene'er I forgather wi' sorrow and care,
I gie them a skelp, as they're creepin' alang,
Wi' a cog o' gude swats, and an auld Scottish sang.

I whyles claw the elbow o' troublesome thought;
But man is a soger, and life is a faught:
My mirth and gude humour are coin in my pouch,
And my freedom's my lairdship nae monarch dare touch.

A towmond o' trouble, should that be my fa'
A night o' gude fellowship sowthers it a';
When at the blythe end of our journey at last,
Wha the deil ever thinks o' the road he has past?

Blind Chance, let her snapper and stoyte on her way,
Be 't to me, be 't frae me, e'en let the jad gae:
Come ease or come travail, come pleasure or pain.
My warst word is — 'Welcome, and welcome again!'

## THE AULD FARMER'S NEW-YEAR
## MORNING SALUTATION TO HIS
## AULD MARE, MAGGIE

A guid New-Year I wish thee, Maggie!
Hae, there's a ripp to thy auld baggie:
Tho' thou's howe-backit now, an' knaggie,
      I've seen the day,
Thou could hae gane like ony staggie
      Out-owre the lay.

Tho' now thou 's dowie, stiff, an' crazy,
An' thy auld hide as white 's a daisie
I've seen thee dappl't, sleek an' glaizie,
      A bonnie gray:
He should been tight that daur't to raize thee,
      Ance in a day.

Thou ance was i' the foremost rank,
A filly buirdly, steeve, an' swank,
An' set weel down a shapely shank,
      As e'er tread yird;
An' could hae flown out-owre a stank,
      Like ony bird.

It's now some nine-an'-twenty year,
Sin' thou was my guid-father's meere;
He gied me thee, o' tocher clear,
      An' fifty mark;
Tho' it was sma', 'twas weel-won gear,
      An' thou was stark.

When first I gaed to woo my Jenny,
Ye then was trottin' wi' your minnie:
Tho' ye was trickie, slee, an' funnie,
                Ye ne'er was donsie:
But hamely, tawie, quiet, an' cannie,
                An' unco sonsie.

That day ye pranc'd wi' muckle pride,
When ye bure hame my bonnie bride;
An' sweet an' gracefu' she did ride,
                Wi' maiden air!
Kyle-Stewart I could braggèd wide
                For sic a pair.

Tho' now ye dow but hoyte and hobble,
An' wintle like a saumont-coble,
That day ye was a jinker noble
                For heels an' win'!
An' ran them till they a' did wauble
                Far, far behin'.

When thou an' I were young and skiegh,
An' stable-meals at fairs were driegh,
How thou wad prance, an' snore an' skriegh
                An' tak the road!
Town's-bodies ran and stood abiegh,
                An' ca't thee mad.

When thou was corn't, an' I was mellow,
We took the road aye like a swallow:
At brooses thou had ne'er a fellow
        For pith an' speed;
But ev'ry tail thou pay't them hollow,
        Whare'er thou gaed.

The sma', droop-rumpl't, hunter cattle,
Might aiblins waur't thee for a brattle;
But sax Scotch miles, thou tried their mettle,
        An' gart them whaizle:
Nae whip nor spur, but just a wattle
        O' saugh or hazel.

Thou was a noble fittie-lan',
As e'er in tug or tow was drawn!
Aft thee an' I, in aucht hours' gaun,
        On guid March-weather,
Hae turn'd sax rood beside our han',
        For days thegither.

Thou never braindg't, an' fetch't, an' fliskit,
But thy auld tail thou wad hae whiskit,
An' spread abreed thy weel-fill'd briskit
        Wi' pith an' pow'r,
Till spritty knowes wad rair't and riskit,
        An' slypet owre.

When frosts lay lang, an' snaws were deep,
An' threaten'd labour back to keep,
I gied thy cog a wee bit heap
   Aboon the timmer;
I kenn'd my Maggie wad na sleep
   For that, or simmer.

In cart or car thou never reestit;
The steyest brae thou wad hae fac't it;
Thou never lap, an' sten't, and breastit,
   Then stood to blaw;
But, just thy step a wee thing hastit,
   Thou snoov't awa.

My pleugh is now thy bairn-time a',
Four gallant brutes as e'er did draw;
Forbye sax mae I've sell't awa
   That thou hast nurst:
They drew me thretteen pund an' twa,
   The vera warst.

Mony a sair darg we twa hae wrought,
An' wi' the weary warl' fought!
An' mony an anxiuos day I thought
   We wad be beat!
Yet here to crazy age we're brought,
   Wi' something yet.

And think na, my auld trusty servan'
That now perhaps thou's less deservin',
An' thy auld days may end in starvin';
      For my last fou,
A heapit stimpart, I'll reserve ane
      Laid by for you.

We've worn to crazy years thegither;
We'll toyte about wi' ane anither;
Wi' tentie care I'll flit thy tether
      To some hain'd rig,
Whare ye may nobly rax your leather,
      Wi' sma' fatigue.

## COMING THROUGH THE RYE

Coming through the rye, poor body,
  Coming through the rye,
She draiglet a' her petticoatie,
  Coming through the rye.

Gin a body meet a body
  Coming through the rye;
Gin a body kiss a body,
  Need a body cry?

Gin a body meet a body
  Coming through the glen;
Gin a body kiss a body,
  Need the world ken?

Jenny's a' wat, poor body;
  Jenny's seldom dry;
She draiglet a' her petticoatie,
  Coming through the rye.

## SCOTCH DRINK

*Extract from Scotch Drink*

*Gie him strong drink, until he wink,*
*    That's sinking in despair;*
*An' liquor guid to fir his bluid,*
*    That's prest wi' grief an' care;*
*There let him bouse, an' deep carouse,*
*    Wi' bumpers flowing o'er,*
*Till he forgets his loves or debts,*
*    An' minds his griefs no more.*
SOLOMON (PROVERBS XXXI. 6,7)

Let other Poets raise a fracas
'Bout vines an' wines, an' drunken Bacchus,
An' crabbèd names an' stories wrack us
            An' grate our lug;
I sing the juice Scotch bear can mak us
            In glass or jug.

O thou, my Muse! guid auld Scotch Drink,
Whether thro' wimplin worms thou jink,
Or, richly brown, ream owre the brink,
            In glorious faem,
Inspire me, till I lisp an' wink,
            To sing thy name!

Let husky wheat the haughs adorn,
An' aits set up their awnie horn,
An' pease an' beans at een or morn,
            Perfume the plain;
Leeze me on thee, John Barleycorn,
            Thou King o' grain!

On thee aft Scotland chows her cood,
In souple scones, the wale o' food!
Or tumblin' in the boiling flood
        Wi' kail an' beef;
But when thou pours thy strong heart's blood,
        There thou shines chief.

Food fills the wame, an' keeps us livin';
Tho' life's a gift no worth receivin'
When heavy-dragg'd wi' pine an' grievin';
        But oil'd by thee,
The wheels o' life gae down-hill, scrievin'
        Wi' rattlin' glee.

Thou clears the head o' doited Lear;
Thou cheers the heart o' drooping Care;
Thou strings the nerves o' Labour sair,
        At's weary toil;
Thou even brightens dark Despair
        Wi' gloomy smile.

Aft, clad in massy siller weed,
Wi' gentles thou erects thy head;
Yet humbly kind, in time o' need,
        The poor man's wine,
His wee drap parritch, or his bread,
        Thou kitchens fine.

Thou art the life o' public haunts;
But thee, what were our fairs and rants?
Ev'n godly meetings o' the saunts,
       By thee inspir'd
When gaping they beseige the tents,
       Are doubly fir'd.

That merry night we get the corn in!
O sweetly then thou reams the horn in!
Or reekin' on a New-Year mornin'
       In cog or bicker,
An' just a wee drap sp'ritual burn in,
       An' gusty sucker!

When Vulcan gies his bellows breath,
An' ploughmen gather wi' their graith,
O rare to see thee fizz an' freath
       I' th' luggèd caup!
Then Burnewin comes on like death
       At ev'ry chaup.

Nae mercy, then, for airn or steel;
The brawnie, banie, ploughman chiel
Brings hard owrehip, wi' sturdy wheel,
       The strong forehammer,
Till block an' studdie ring an' reel
       Wi' dinsome clamour.

When skirlin' weanies see the light,
Thou maks the gossips clatter bright
How fumblin' cuifs their dearies slight -
           Wae worth the name!
Nae Howdie get a social night,
           Or plack frae them.

When neibors angers at a plea,
An' just as wud as wud can be,
How easy can the barley-bree
           Cement the quarrel!
It's aye the cheapest lawyer's fee
           To taste the barrel.

Alake! that e'er my Muse has reason
To wyte her countrymen wi' treason;
But mony daily weet their weasan'
           Wi' liquors nice,
An' hardly, in a winter's season,
           E'er spier her price.

Wae worth that brandy, burning trash!
Fell source o' mony a pain an' brash!
Twins mony a poor, doylt, drucken hash
           O' half his days;
An' sends, beside, auld Scotland's cash
           To her warst faes.

Ye Scots, wha wish auld Scotland well,
Ye chief, to you my tale I tell,
Por plackless devils like mysel'!
   It sets you ill,
Wi' bitter, dearthfu' wines to mell,
    Or foreign gill.

May gravels round his blather wrench,
An' gouts torment him, inch by inch,
Wha twists his gruntle wi' a glunch
   O' sour disdain,
Out owre a glass o' whisky punch
    Wi' honest men! .....

## HIGHLAND MARY

Ye banks, and braes, and streams around
      The castle o' Montgomery,
Green be your woods, and fair your flowers,
      Your waters never drumlie!
There simmer first unfauld her robes,
      And there the langest tarry;
For there I took the last fareweel
      O' my sweet Highland Mary.

How sweetly bloom'd the gay green birk,
      How rich the hawthorn's blossom
As underneath their fragrant shade
      I clasp'd her to my bosom!
The golden hours on angels wings
      Flew o'er me and my dearie;
For dear to me as light and life
      Was my sweet Highland Mary

Wi' mony a vow, and lock'd embrace,
      Our parting was fu' tender;
And, pledging aft to meet again,
      We tore oursels asunder;
But oh! fell death's untimely frost,
      That nipt my flower sae early!
Now green's the sod, and cauld's the clay,
      That wraps my Highland Mary!

THE PARTING OF ROBERT BURNS AND HIS MARY

O pale, pale now, those rosy lips,
    I aft have kiss'd sae fondly!
And closed for aye the sparkling glance,
    That dwelt on me sae kindly!
And mould'ring now in silent dust,
    That heart that lo'ed me dearly!
But still within my bosom's core
    Shall live my Highland Mary.

## JOHN ANDERSON, MY JO

John Anderson my jo, John,
    When we were first acquent,
Your locks were like the raven,
    Your bonnie brow was brent;
But now your brow is beld, John,
    Your locks are like the snaw;
But blessings on your frosty pow,
    John Andreson, my jo.

John Anderson my jo, John,
    We clamb the hill thegither;
And mony a canty day, John,
    We've had wi' ane anither:
Now we maun totter down, John,
    And hand in hand we'll go,
And sleep thegither at the foot,
    John Anderson, my jo.

## TO MARY IN HEAVEN

Thou lingering star, with lessening ray,
    That lov'st to greet the early morn,
Again thou usherest in the day
    My Mary from my soul was torn.
O Mary! dear departed shade!
    Where is thy place of blissful rest?
Seest thou thy lover lowly laid?
    Hear'st thou the groans that rend his breast?

That sacred hour can I forget?
    Can I forget the hallow'd grove,
Where by winding Ayr we met,
    To live one day of parting love?
Eternity will not efface
    Those records dear of transports past;
Thy image at our last embrace –
    Ah! little thought we 'twas our last!

Ayr gurgling kiss'd his pebbled shore,
    O'erhung with wild woods, thickening green;
The fragrant birch, and hawthorn hoar,
    Twin'd amorous round the raptur'd scene.
The flowers sprang wanton to be prest,
    The birds sang love on ev'ry spray,
Till too too soon, the glowest west
    Proclaim'd the speed of wingèd day.

Still o'er these scenes my memory wakes,
    And fondly broods with miser care!
Time but the impression deeper makes,
    As streams their channels deeper wear.
My Mary, dear departed shade!
    Where is they blissful place of rest?
Seest thou thy lover lowly laid?
    Hear'st thou the groans that rend his breast?


## TO A MOUNTAIN DAISY

Wee modest crimson-tippèd flow'r,
Thou 's met me in an evil hour;
For I maun crush amang the stoure
              Thy slender stem:
To spare thee now is past my pow'r,
              Thou bonnie gem.

Alas! it 's no thy neibor sweet,
The bonnie lark, companion meet,
Bending thee 'mang the dewy weet
              Wi' spreckl'd breast,
When upward-springing, blythe, to greet
              The purpling east.

Cauld blew the bitter-biting north
Upon thy early humble birth;
Yet cheerfully thou glinted forth
              Amid the storm,
Scarce rear'd above the parent-earth
              Thy tender form.

The flaunting flow'rs our gardens yield
High shelt'ring woods and wa's maun shield,
But thou, beneath the random bield
                O' clod or stane,
Adorns the histie stibble-field,
                Unseen, alane.

There, in thy scanty mantle clad,
Thy snawy bosom sun-ward spread,
Thou lifts thy unassuming head
                In humble guise;
But now the share uptears thy bed
                And low thou lies!

Such is the fate of artless maid,
Sweet flow'ret of the rural shade,
By love's simplicity betray'd
                And guileless trust,
Till she like thee, all soil'd, is laid
                Low i' the dust.

Such is the fate of simple bard,
On life's rough ocean luckless starr'd:
Unskilful he to note the card
                Of prudent lore,
Till billows rage, and gales blow hard,
                And whelm him o'er!

Such fate to suffering worth is giv'n,
Who long with wants and woes has striv'n,
By human pride or cunning driv'n
                To mis'ry's brink,
Till wrench'd of ev'ry stay but Heav'n
                He, ruin'd, sink

Ev'n thou who mourn'st the Daisy's fate,
That fate is thine — no distant date;
Stern Ruin's ploughshare drives elate
                              Full on thy bloom
Till crush'd beneath the furrow's weight
                              Shall be thy doom!


## LINES ON MEETING WITH
## LORD DAER

This wot ye all whom it concerns,
I, Rhymer Robin, alias Burns,
                October twenty-third,
A ne'er to be forgotten day,
Sae far I sprachled up the brae,
                I dinner'd wi' a Lord.

I've been at druken writers' feasts,
Nay, been bitch-fou 'mang godly priests,
                Wi' rev'rence be it spoken!
I've even join'd the honour'd jorum,
When mighty Squireships of the quorum,
                Their hydra drouth did sloken.

But wi' a Lord! — stand out my shin;
A Lord — a Peer — an Earl's son,
                Up higher yet, my bonnet!
And sic a Lord! — lang Scotch ells twa,
Our Peerage he o'erlooks them a',
                As I look o'er my sonnet.

But O for Hogarth's magic pow'r!
To show Sir Bardie's willyart glow'r,
       And how he star'd and stammer'd,
When goavin, as if his led wi' branks,
An' stumpin on his ploughman shanks,
       He in the parlour hammer'd.

I sidling shelter'd in a nook,
An' at his Lordship steal't a look,
       Like some potentous omen;
Except good-sense and social glee,
An' (what surprised me) modesty,
       I markèd nought uncommon.

I watch'd the symptoms o' the Great,
The gentle pride, the lordly state,
       The arrogant assuming;
The fient a pride, nae pride had he,
Nor sauce, nor state that I could see,
       Mair than an honest ploughman.

Then from his lordship I shall learn
Henceforth to meet with unconcern
       One rank as well's another;
Nae honest worthy man need care
To meet with noble youthful Daer,
       For he but meets a brother.

## OF A' THE AIRTS

Of a' the airts the wind can blaw,
  I dearly like the west,
For there the bonnie lassie lives,
   The lassie I lo'e best:
There's wild woods grow, and rivers row,
   And mony a hill between;
But day and night my fancy's flight
   Is ever wi' my Jean.

I see her in the dewy flowers,
   I see her sweet and fair:
I hear her in the tunefu' birds,
   I hear her charm the air:
There's not a boonie flower that springs
   By fountain, shaw, or green;
There's not a bonnie bird that sings,
   But minds me o' my Jean.

FOR A' THAT AND A' THAT

Is there, for honest poverty,
    That hangs his head, and a' that?
The coward-slave, we pass him by,
    We dare be poor for a' that!
        For a' that, and a' that;
            Our toils obscure, and a' that;
            The rank is but the guinea's stamp;
                The man's the gowd for a' that.

What tho' on hamely fare we dine,
    Wear hodden-gray, and a' that;
Gie fools their silks, and knaves their wine.
    A man 's a man for a' that.
        For a' that, and a' that,
            Their tinsel show, and a' that;
            That honest man, tho' e'er sae poor,
                Is King o' men for a' that.

Ye see yon birkie, ca'd a lord,
    Wha struts, and stares, and a' that;
Tho' hundreds worship at his word,
    He's but a coof for a' that:
        For a' that, and a' that,
          His riband, star, and a' that,
        The man of independent mind,
          He looks and laughs at a' that.

A prince can mak a belted knight,
    A marquis, duke, and a' that;
But an honest man's aboon his might,
    Guid faith he mauna fa' that!
        For a' that, and a' that,
          Their dignties, and a' that,
        The pith o' sense, and pride o' worth,
          Are higher rank than a' that.

Then let us pray that come it may,
    As come it will for a' that,
That sense and worth, o'er a' the earth,
    May bear the gree, and a' that,
        For a' that and a' that,
          It's coming yet, for a' that,
        That man to man the warld o'er
          Shall brithers be for a' that.

## ADDRESS TO THE DEIL

O thou! whatever title suit thee,
Auld Hornie, Satan, Nick, or Clootie,
Wha in yon cavern grim an' sootie,
   Clos'd under hatches,
Spairges about the brunstane cootie,
   To scaud poor wretches!

Hear me, auld Hangie, for a wee,
An' let poor damnèd bodies be;
I'm sure sma' pleasure it can gie,
   Ev'n to a deil,
To skelp an' scaud poor dogs like me,
   An' hear us squeal!

Great is thy pow'r, an' great thy fame;
Far ken'd an' noted is thy name;
An', tho' yon lowin' heuch's thy hame,
   Thou travels far;
An' faith! thou's neither lag nor lame.
   Nor blate nor scaur.
Whyles rangin' like a roarin' lion

For prey, a' holes an' corners tryin';
Whyles on the strong-wing'd tempest flyin',
      Tirlin' the kirks;
Whyles, in the human bosom pryin',
        Unseen thou lurks.

I've heard my reverend graunie say,
In lanely glens ye like to stray;
Or, where auld ruin'd castles gray
      Nod to the moon,
Ye fright the nightly wand'rer's way,
        Wi' eldritch croon

When twilight did my graunie summon
To say her pray'rs, douce, honest woman!
Aft yont the dyke she's heard you bummin',
      Wi' eerie drone;
Or rustlin', thro' the boortrees comin',
        Wi' heavy groan.

Ae dreary, windy, winter night
The stars shot down wi' sklentin' light,
Wi' you, mysel, I gat a fright
      Ayont the lough;
Ye like a rash-buss stood in sight
        Wi' waving sough.

The cudgel in my nieve did shake,
Each bristled hair stood like a stake,
When wi' an eldritch, stoor 'quaick, quaick,'
      Amang the springs,
Awa ye squatter'd like a drake,
        On whistlin' wings.

Let warlocks grim an' wither'd hags
Tell how wi' you on ragweed nags
They skim the muirs, an' dizzy crags
      Wi' wicked speed;
And in kirk-yards renew their leagues
      Owre howkit dead.

Thence country wives, wi' toil an' pain,
May plunge an' plunge the kirn in vain;
For oh! the yellow treasure's taen
      By witchin' skill;
An' dawtit, twal-pint Hawkie's gane
      As yell's the bill.

Thence mystic knots mak great abuse
On young guidmen, fond, keen, an' crouse
When the best wark-lume i' the house,
      By cantrip wit,
Is instant made no worth a louse,
      Just at the bit.

When thowes dissolve the snawy hoord,
An' float the jinglin' icy-boord,
Then water-kelpies haunt the foord,
      By your direction,
An' 'nighted trav'lers are allur'd
      To their destruction.

An' aft your moss-traversing spunkies
Decoy the wight that late an' drunk is:
The bleezin, curst, mischievous monkies
      Delude his eyes,
Till in some miry slough he sunk is,
      Ne'er mair to rise.

When mason's mystic word an' grip
In storms an' tempest raise you up,
Some cock or cat your rage maun stop,
        Or, strange to tell!
The youngest brither ye wad whip
        Aff straught to hell.

Lang syne, in Eden's bonnie yard,
When youthfu' lovers first were pair'd,
And all the soul of love they shar'd,
        The raptur'd hour,
Sweet on the fragrant flow'ry swaird,
        In shady bow'r;

Then you, ye auld snick-drawing dog!
Ye cam to Paradise incog,
An' play'd on man a cursed brogue,
        (Black be you fa!)
An' gied the infant warld a shog,
        'Maist ruin'd a'.

D'ye mind that day, when in a bizz,
Wi' reekit duds, an' reestit gizz,
Ye did present your smoutie phiz
        'Mang better folk,
An' sklented on the man of Uzz
        Your spitefu' joke?

An' how ye gat him i' your thrall,
An' brak him out o' house an' hal',
While scabs an' botches did him gall
        Wi' bitter claw,
An' lows'd his ill-tongu'd wicked scaul,
        Was warst ava?

But a' your doings to rehearse,
Your wily snares an' fechtin' fierce,
Sin' that day Michael did you pierce,
        Down to this time,
Wad ding a' Lallan tongue, or Erse,
        In prose or rhyme.

An' now auld Cloots, I ken ye're thinkin'
A certain Bardie's rantin', drinkin',
Some luckless hour will send hem linkin',
        To your black pit;
But faith! he'll turn a corner jinkin',
        An' cheat you yet.

But fare you weel, auld Nickie-ben!
O wad ye tak a thought an' men'!
Ye aiblins might–I dinna ken–
        Still hae a stake:
I'm wae to think upo' yon den,
        Ev'n for your sake!

## A RED, RED ROSE

O, My Luve's like a red, red rose
   That's newly sprung in June:
O, my Luve's like the melodie
   That's sweetly played in tune!

As fair art thou, my bonnie lass,
   So deep in luve am I;
And I will luve thee still, my dear,
   Till a' the seas gang dry:

Till a' the seas gang dry, my dear,
   And the rocks melt wi' the sun;
I will luve thee still my dear,
   While the sands o' life shall run.

And fare thee weel, my only Luve!
   And fare thee weel a while!
And I will come again, my Luve,
   Tho' it were ten thousand mile.

## AULD LANG SYNE

Should auld acquaintance be forgot,
  And never brought to mind?
Should auld acquaintance be forgot,
  And auld lang syne?

For auld lang syne, my dear.
  For auld lang syne,
We'll tak a cup o' kindness yet,
  For auld lang syne.

And surely ye'll be your pint-stowp,
  And surely I'll be mine;
And we'll tak a cup o' kindness yet
  For auld lang syne.

We twa hae run about the braes,
  And pu'd the gowans fine;
But we've wander'd mony a weary fit
  Sin' auld lang syne.

We twa hae paidled i' the burn,
  From morning sun till dine;
But seas between us braid hae roar'd
  Sin' auld lang syne.

And there's a hand, my trusty fiere,
  And gie's a hand o' thine;
And we'll tak a right guid-willie waught,
  For auld lang syne.

## HOLY WILLIE'S PRAYER

O Thou, wha in the Heavens dost dwell,
Wha, as it pleases best thysel',
Sends ane to heaven and ten to hell,
       A' for thy glory,
And no for ony guid or ill
       They've done afore thee!

I bless and praise thy matchless might,
Whan thousands thou hast left in night,
That I am here afore thy sight,
       For gifts an' grace
A burnin' an' a shinin' light,
       To a' this place.

What was I, or my generation,
That I should get sic exaltation?
I, wha deserve most just damnation,
       For broken laws,
Sax thousand years 'fore my creation,
       Thro' Adam's cause.

When frae my mither's womb I fell,
Thou might hae plungèd me in hell,
To gnash my gums, to weep and wail,
       In burning lakes,
Where damnèd devils roar and yell,
       Chain'd to their stakes;

Yet I am here a chosen sample,
To show thy grace is great and ample;
I'm here a pillar in thy temple,
                    Strong as a rock,
A guide, a buckler, an example
                    To a' thy flock.

O Lord, thou kens what zeal I bear,
When drinkers drink, and swearers swear,
And singin' there and dancin' here,
                    Wi' great an' sma':
For I am keepit by thy fear
                    Free frae them a'.

But yet, O' Lord! confess I must
At times I'm fash'd wi' fleshly lust;
An' sometimes too, in warldly trust,
                    Vile self gets in;
But thou remembers we are dust,
                    Defil'd in sin.

O Lord! yestreen, thou kens, wi' Meg -
Thy pardon I sincerely beg;
O! may't ne'er be a livin' plague
                    To my dishonour,
An' I'll ne'er lift a lawless leg
                    Again upon her.

Besides I farther maun allow,
Wi' Lizzie's lass, three times I trow -
But, Lord, that Friday I was fou,
                    When I cam near her,
Or else thou kens thy servant true
                    Wad never steer her.

May be thou lets this fleshly thorn
Beset thy servant e'en and morn
Lest he owre high and proud should turn,
          That he's sae gifted;
If sae, thy hand maun e'en be borne,
          Until thou lift it.

Lord, bless thy chosen in this place,
For here thou hast a chosen race;
But God confound their stubborn face,
          And blast their name,
Wha bring thy elders to disgrace
          An' public shame.

Lord, mind Gawn Hamilton's deserts,
He drinks, an' swears, an' plays at cartes,
Yet has sae mony takin' arts
          Wi' grit an' sma',
Frae God's ain priest the people's hearts
          He steals awa'.

An' when we chasten'd him therefor,
Thou kens how he bred sic a splore
As set the warld in a roar
          O' laughin' at us;
Curse thou his basket and his store,
          Kail and potatoes.

Lord, hear my earnest cry and pray'r
Against that presbyt'ry o' Ayr;
Thy strong right hand, Lord, make it bare
          Upo' their heads;
Lord; weigh it down, and dinna spare,
          For their misdeeds.

O Lord my God, that glib-tongu'd Aiken
My very heart and soul are quakin',
To think how we stood sweatin', shakin',
    An' piss'd wi' dread,
While he, wi hingin' lip and snakin',
    Held up his head.

Lord, in the day of vengeance try him;
Lord, visit them wha did employ him,
And pass not in thy mercy by them,
    Nor hear their pray'r:
But, for thy people's sake destroy them,
    And dinna spare.

But, Lord, remember me and mine
Wi' mercies temp'ral and divine,
That I for gear and grace may shine
    Excell'd by nane,
And a' the glory shall be thine,
    Amen, Amen!

RIVER DOON

## YE BANKS AND BRAES
## O' BONNIE DOON

Ye banks and braes o' bonnie Doon,
   How can ye bloom sae fresh and fair?
How can ye chant, ye little birds,
   And I sae weary fu' o' care?
Thou'lt break my heart, thou warbling bird,
   That wantons thro' the flowering thorn:
Thou minds me o' departed joys,
   Departed never to return.

Aft hae I rov'd by bonnie Doon,
   To see the rose and woodbine twine;
And ilka bird sang o' its love,
   And fondly sae did I o' mine.
Wi' lightsome heart I pu'd a rose,
   Fu' sweet upon its thorny tree;
And my fause lover stole my rose,
   But ah! he left the thorn wi' me.

## THE GLOOMY NIGHT IS
## GATHERING FAST

THE gloomy night is gathering fast,
Loud roars the wild inconstant blast,
Yon murky cloud is foul with rain,
I see it driving o'er the plain;
The hunter now has left the moor,
The scatter'd coveys meet secure,
While here I wander, prest with care,
Along the lonely banks of Ayr.

The Autumn mourns her ripening corn
By early Winter's ravage torn;
Across her placid azure sky,
She sees the scowling tempest fly:
Chill runs my blood to hear it rave,
I think upon the stormy wave,
Where many a danger I must dare,
Far from the bonnie banks of Ayr.

'Tis not the surging billow's roar,
'Tis not that fatal, deadly shore;
Tho' death in ev'ry shape appear,
The wretched have no more to fear:
But round my heart the ties are bound,
That heart transpierc'd with many a wound:
These bleed afresh, those ties I tear,
To leave the bonnie banks of Ayr.

Farewell, old Coila's hills and dales,
Her heathy moors and winding vales;
The scenes where wretched fancy roves,
Pursuing past unhappy loves!
Farewell, my friends! Farewell, my foes!
My peace with these, my love with those;
The bursting tears my heart declare,
Farewell, the bonnie banks of Ayr!

## WHISTLE, AND I'LL COME TO YOU, MY LAD

O whistle, and I'll come to you, my lad;
O whistle, and I'll come to you, my lad:
Tho' father and mither and a' should gae mad,
O whistle, and I'll come to you, my lad.

But warily tent, when ye come to court me,
And come na unless the back-yett be a-jee;
Syne up the back-stile, and let naebody see,
And come as ye were na comin' to me.
And come as ye were na comin' to me.

At kirk, or at market, whene'er ye meet me,
Gang by me as tho' that ye car'd na a flee:
But steal me a blink o' your bonnie black ee,
Yet look as ye were na lookin' at me.
Yet look as ye were na lookin' at me.

Aye vow and protest that ye care na for me,
And whiles ye may lightly my beauty a wee;
But court na anither, tho' jokin' ye be,
For fear that she wyle your fancy frae me.
For fear that she wyle your fancy frae me.

## BURNS NIGHT

Celebrated on the 25th January each year, the anniversary of
Burn's birthday, a typical 'Burns Nicht' usually opens with the
'Selkirk Grace', attributed to Burns:

> Some hae meat, and canna eat,
> And some wad eat that want it,
> But we hae meet and we can eat,
> And sae the Lord be thankit.

> The meal then served would be:
> *Cock-a-Leekie soup*
> *Haggis with Tatties-an'-Neeps*
> *Roastit beef*
> *Tipsy Laird*
> *Dunlop Cheese*

A member of the party would address the haggis, quoting the
poem *Address To a Haggis*. Then the poet is toasted with whisky.
During the evening various other Burns poems and songs can
be recited, and toasts made 'to the Ladies', 'to the Gentleman'
and 'to our land'.

## ADDRESS TO A HAGGIS

Fair fa' your honest, sonsie face,
Great chieftian o' the pudding-race!
Aboon them a' ye tak your place,
                              Painch, tripe, or thairm:
Weel are ye wordy o' a grace
                              A lang's my arm.

The groaning trencher there ye fill,
Your hurdies like a distant hill,
Your pin wad help to mend a mill
                              In time o' need,
While thro' your pores the dews distil
                              Like amber bead.

His knife sees rustic labour dight,
An' cut you up with ready sleight,
Trenching your gushing entrails bright,
                              Like onie ditch;
And then, O what a glorious sight,
                              Warm-reekin, rich!

Then horn for horn, they stretch an' strive,
Deil tak the hindmost! on they drive,
Till a' their weel-swall'd kytes belyve
                              Are bent like drums;
Then auld Guidman, maist like to rive,
                              Bethankit hums.

Is there that o'er his French *ragout,*
Or *olio* that wad staw a sow,
Or *fricassee* wad make her spew
                              Wi' perfect sconner,
Looks down wi' sneering, scornful view
                              On sic dinner?

Poor devil! see him owre his trash,
As feckless as a wither'd rash,
His spindle shank, a guid whip-lash,
                              His nieve a nit;
Thro' bloody flood or field to dash,
                              O how unfit!

But mark the rustic, *haggis-fed,*
The trembling earth resounds his tread,
Clap in his walie nieve a blade,
                              He'll mak it whissle;
An' legs an' arms, an' heads will send,
                              Like taps o' thrissle.

Ye powers, wha mak mankind your care,
And dish them out their bill o' fare,
Auld Scotland wants nae skinking ware
                              That jaups in luggies;
But, if ye wish her gratefu' prayer,
                              Gie her a *Haggis!*

## EPITATH FOR JAMES SMITH

Lament him, Mauchline husbands a',
    He aften did assist ye;
For had ye staid hale weeks awa,
    Your wives they ne'er had miss'd ye.

Ye Mauchline bairns, as on ye pass
    To school in bands thegither,
O tread ye lightly on his grass, –
    Perhaps he was your father!

## EPITATH FOR WILLIAM NICOL,
## OF THE HIGH SCHOOL,
## EDINBURGH

Ye maggots, feed on Nicol's brain,
    For few sic feasts you've gotten;
And fix your claws in Nicol's heart,
    For deil a bit o't's rotten.

## EPITATH FOR ROBERT AIKEN, ESQ

Know thou, O stranger to the fame
Of this much lov'd, much honoured name!
(For none that knew him need be told)
A warmer heart death ne'er made cold.

## Select Bibliography

David Daiches, *Robert Burns, revised edition* (London and New York 1966)

De Lancey Ferguson (ed.), *The Letters of Robert Burns, 2 vols* (Oxford 1931)

De Lancey Ferguson, *Pride and Passion: Robert Burns 1759-1796* (New York 1939)

Maurice Lindsay, *The Burns Encyclopaedia, 2nd revised edition* (London 1970)

F B Snyder, *The Life of Robert Burns* (New York 1932)

Hugh MacDiarmid, *Burns Today and Tomorrow* (Edinburgh 1959)

Alan Bold, *A Burns Companion* (London 1991)

# GLOSSARY

A
abiegh, *aloof*
aboon the timmer, *above the wooden (edge)*
a-gley, *wide of the aim*
aiblins, *perhaps*
airns, *irons*
airts, *regions of the earth or sky*
a-jee, *ajar*
a-steerin, *moving*

B
bain, *bone*
bairns, *children*
baith, *both*
bannock, *cake of oatmeal bread*
bawsent, *white-streaked*
bear the gree, *win the prize*
beld, *bald*
bickering brattle, *hurrying scamper*
bield, *shelter*
big, *build*
biggin', *building*
bill, *bull*
billies, *fellows*
birkie, *smart fellow*
birks, *birches*
bit, *crisis*
bitch-fou, *very drunk*
bizz, *flurry*
blate, *shy*
blellum, *babbler*
bletherin', *idle-talking*
blink, *glance*
blinkin', *shining*
blypes, *shreds*
bogles, *hobgoblins*
boortrees, *elder bushes*
bousing, *drinking*
bow-kail, *coleworts with crooked stems*
braindg't, *drew unsteadily*
branks, *a wooden curb*
brattle, *spurt, short race*
braw, *fine, handsome*
brawlie, *well*
breastit, *sprang forward*
breeks, *breeches*
brent, *smooth and straight*
briskit, *breast*

brock, *badger*
brogue, *affront*
brooses, *wedding races to the bride's house*
buirdly, *stalwart*
burdies, *girls*
bum-clock, *humming beetle*
brunstane, *brimstone*
Burnewin, *i.e. burn the wind, a blacksmith*
byke, *hive*

C
ca', *drive*
ca'd a shoe on, *shod*
cairn, *a loose heap of stones*
cannie, *gentle, mild*
cantrip, *charm, a spell*
canty, *merry*
car'd...boddle, *cared not a farthing for devils*
carlin, *witch*
chaup, *a blow*
chiel, *young fellow*
clachan, *a hamlet*
claes, *clothes*
claith, *cloth*
claught, *clutched*
claw, *scratch*
cleekit, *linked arms*
clootie, *hoofie*
coft, *bought*
cog, *wooden bowl*
company bear, *barley*
coof, *a blockhead, a ninny, dolt*
coost her duddies, *cast off her rags*
cootie, *large wooden dish*
cookit, *appeared and disappeared by fits*
coost, *cast*
core, *corps*
couthie, *lovingly*
cowpit, *tumbled*
crackin' crouse, *chatting complacently*
cracks, *talk, chats*
cranreuch, *hoar-frost*
creeshie flannen, *greasy flannel*
croon, *hollow moan*
crooning, *humming*
crouse, *confident*
crummock, *crooked-staff*
cuifs, *blockheads, ninnies*
cutty, *short*

D
daimen-icker, *odd ear of corn*
dawitt, *petted*
devil's pictur'd beuks, *cards*
dine, *dinner-time*
ding, *beat*
dirl, *vibrate*
dizzen, *dozen (reels)*
donsie, *vicious*
dowie, *spiritless*
doylt, *stupid*
drab, *drop*
draiglit, *draggled*
driegh, *tedious*
droop-rumpl't, *with small buttocks*
drouthy, *thirsty*
drumlie, *muddy*
drumly, *turbid*
drunt, *pet*
dub, *puddle*
duddie, *ragged*
duddies, *garments*
dyke, *dry stone wall*

E
eldritch, *ghastly*
erse, *gaelic*
ettle, *purpose*
eydent, *diligent*

F
fa', *lot, lay claim to*
faem, *foam*
fairing, *a present*
fash'd, *troubled*
fawsont, *orderly*
feat, *spruce*
fecht wi' nowt, *fight with cattle, bull-fight*
fell, *pungent*
ferlie, *marvel*
fetch't, *stopped suddenly and then*
fidg'd, *fidgeted*
fient haet, *the devil a one*
fiere, *companion*
fit, *foot*
fittie-lan', *near horse*
  *of the hindmost pair in the plough*
flee, *fly*

fliskit, *fretted at the yoke*
flit, *shift*
fou, *bushel*
foughten, *troubled, driven*
fyke, *fret*

G
gabs, *bold speeches, mouth, jaws*
gae, *to go*
gang awa, *go away*
gars me greet, *makes me weep*
garten, *garters*
gash, *wise*
gate, *way (home)*
gawsie, *flourishing*
gin, *if*
glaizie, *smooth, glossy*
glinted, *peeped*
gloamin, *twilight*
goavin, *looking aimlessly about*
gowans, *flowers of daisies, dandelions,*
  *hawk-weeds etc.*
gowd, *gold*
grape, *grope*
grushie, *of thriving growth*
guid, *good*
guid-father's, *father-in-law's*
guidmen, *husbands*
guid-willie waught, *hearty draught*
gully, *large knife*

H
haffets, *temples*
hafflins, *half*
hain'd rig, *spared ridge*
hallan, *partition-wall*
han'darg, *labour of his hands*
harn, *coarse cloth*
haud, *hold, celebrate*
haurlin', *peeling*
hav'rel, *half-witted*
haw, *copse*
hawkie, *white faced cow*
hecht, *promised*
heft, *haft*
herd, *herd-boy*
her lane, *by herself*
histie, *dry, barren*

hodden-gray, *undyed homespun*
hoordit, *hoarded*
hotch'd, *turned topsy-turvy,*
houlets, *owls*
howe-backit, *hollow-backed*
howkit, *unearthed*
hoy't, *kept urging*
hoyte, *amble crazily*
hurdies, *buttocks*

I
ilka, *every*
indentin, *indenturing*
ither, *other*

J
jauk, *trifle*
jinker noble, *noble goer*
jinkin', *dodging*
jo, *sweetheart*
joctelegs, *clasp-knives*

K
kain, *rents in kind*
kale-runt, *the stem of colewort*
kebbuck, *cheese*
keeks, *peeps*
kirn, *churn*
kittlin, *kitten*
kirns, *harvest-homes*
knaggie, *lean and bony*
kye, *cows*
kythe, *reveal*

L
laith, *loath*
laithfu', *bashful*
lallan, *lowland*
lang syne, *long ago*
lap the hool, *leapt out of her skin*
lav'rock-height, *lark-high*
lays, *leas*
leal, *loyal*
leister, *three pronged dart for striking fish*
lift, *sky*
lightly, *disparage*
limmer, *mistress*
linkin', *hurrying*

linkit, *went at top speed*
linn, *waterfall*
lint i' the bell, *flax in flower*
loan, *lane*
loot a winze, *let (uttered) a curse*
louping, *leaping*
loun, *rascal*
lows'd, *let loose*
luggies, *small wooden dishes*
lugs, *ears*
lum, *chimney*
lunt, *steams*
lyart, *grey*

M
mair, *more*
maun, *must*
mawin, *mowing*
meikle, *as much*
melder, *load of corn sent to be ground*
messan, *mongrel*
midden-hole, *gutter at the bottom*
  *of the dung hill*
minnie, *mother*
mislear'd, *mischievous, unmannerly*
moudieworts, *moles*
muckle, *great, big, much*
murk, *dark, night*

N
naig, *horse*
nappy, *strong ale*
nits, *nuts*

O
or, *ere*
outler quey, *young cow lying by night*
owre, *over, too*

P
pack and thick, *confidentially intimate*
paidl'd, *paddled*
painch, *paunch*
parritch, *porridge*
pattle, *plough-staff*
pechan, *stomach*
pickle, *a small quantity*
pit, *put*

pleugh, *plough-team*
poind, *distrain*
poortith's, *poverty's*
pow, *head*
primsie, *affectedly nice*
pussie's, *the hare's*

Q
queans, *young women*

R
ragweed nags, *ragwort (used as) horses*
rair, *roar*
raize, *rouse*
rantin, *rollicking*
rape, *rope*
rash-buss, *clump of rushes*
rax, *stretch*
ream, *foam*
reaming swats, *frothing ale*
reekit duds, *smoky rags*
reeks, *smokes, steams*
reestit, *was restive*
reestit gizz, *shrivelled wig*
rigwoodie, *withered, lean*
ripp, *handful of unthreshed corn*
riskit, *cracked*
row, *roll*
rowth, *abundance*
rowtin, *lowing*
run de'ils, *downright devils*

S
sair, *sore; to serve*
saumont-coble, f*lat boat used in
 spearing salmon*
sark, *shirt*
saugh, *willow*
sawin, *sowing*
scar, *cliff, bank*
scaur, *scare, afraid*
scawl, *scold (wife)*
scrievin', *running swiftly*
seventeen hunder, *woven in a reed
 of 1,700 divisions; very fine*
shaws, *copes*
sheugh, *ditch*
shog, *shock*
sic, *such*
sicker, *sure, steady*

siller, *silver, money*
skaith, *to damage, to injure, injury*
skellum, *worthless fellow*
skelp, *slap*
skelpit, *pounded*
skiegh, *mettlesome*
sklented, *cast with sinister purpose*
sklentin, *ominous*
skriech, *screech*
skriegh, *neigh*
skirl, *scream*
slade, *slid*
slaps, *gaps in a fence*
slee, *sly*
sloken, *quench*
slypet owre, *fallen smoothly over*
smiddie, *smithy*
smoor'd, *smothered*
smytrie, *a numerous company*
snapper, *stumble*
snash, *abuse*
sneeshin'-mill, *snuff box*
snell, *biting*
snick-drawing, *trick-contriving*
snoov't awa, *went steadily on*
snore, *snort*
snowkit, *examined by sniffing*
sonsie, *good-natured*
sough, *a sigh, a sound dying on the ear*
souple, *supple*
souter, *shoemaker*
sow'ns, *flummery of oats*
sowpe, *sup, spoonful (of milk)*
sowther, *solder, patch up*
spairges, *splashes*
spean, *wean (by disgust)*
spier, *to ask*
spiers, *inquiries*
spleuchan, *a tobacco-pouch*
splore, *a frolic, noise, riot*
sprachled, *clambered*
spritty knowes, *hillocks full of spit (rush) roots*
spunkies, *will-o'-the-wisps*
squatter'd, *fluttered in the water*
stacher, *to stagger*
staggie, *young horse*
stane, *stone*
stank, *pool of standing water*
stap, *stop*
staw, *stole*

stechin', *cramming*
steek, *shut*
steeks, *stiches*
steer, *molest*
steeve, *firm*
sten't, *reared*
stents, *dues*
steyest, *steepest*
stimpart, *eighth part of a bushel*
stoor, *harsh*
stoure, *dust*
stoyte, *stagger*
strae-death, *to die in bed*
stroan't, *made water*
strunt, *liquor*
stoure, *dust*
sturt, *fret*
swank, *limber*
swats, *new ale*
swirlie, *twisted*

T
tassie, *goblet*
tawie, *easy to handle*
tawted tyke, *matted cur*
twal-pint Hawkie, *cow yielding twelve
 pints at a milking*
tent, *heed*
tentie, *heedful*
timmer, *woods*
tippenny, *twopenny (ale)*
thack and rape, *thatch and rope*
thegither, *together*
the lave, *the rest*
thir breeks, *these breeches*
thole, *endure*
thowes, *thaws*
thrang, *busy*
thrave, *twenty-four sheaves*
three-tae'd, *three pronged*
throu'ther, *pell-mell*
thy bairn-time a', *all thy offspring*
thy lane, *by thyself*
tirlin', *stripping*
tocher, *marriage-portion*
toom, *empty*
touzie, *rough, shaggy*
towmond, *twelve-month*
toyte, *totter*
timmer-propt for thrawin', *propped
 with timber against warping*
trow, *believe*

tug, *thongs of hide*
twal, *twelve*

U
unco, *strange*
uncos, *wonders, news*
usquabae, *whiskey*

V
vauntie, *in high spirits*

W
wabster, *weaver*
wad, *bet*
wale, *choose*
walie, *ample, large*
wame, *belly*
wark, *work*
wark-lume, *tool*

wattle, *wand*
wauble, *wobble*
waur't, *worsted*
wawlie, *large, plump*
weans, *children*
wee blastit wonner, *tiny damn'd marvel*
weel-hain'd, *well-saved*
whaizle, *wheeze*
whalpit, *whelped*
whins, *furze*
whyles, *whiles, sometimes*
wiel,*eddy*
willyart glow'r, *bewildered stare*
wimplin', *winding, meandering*
wimpl't, *meandered*
wintle, *lurch*
winn/winnow, *to win*
winnock-bunker, *window-seat*
wooer-babs, *love-knots*

writers', *lawyers'*
wud, *mad*
wyte, *blame*

Y
yard, *garden*
yell, *milkless*
ye'll be, *you'll be good for*
yestreen, *yesternight*
yett, *gate*
yird, *earth*
'yont, *beyond*